CLIMB CAPITOL HILL

THE INSIDE SCOOP ON
U.S. CONGRESS

WRITTEN BY TED ANDERSON

ILLUSTRATED BY LUIZ FERNANDO DA SILVA

CAPSTONE PRESS
a capstone imprint

Published by Capstone Press, an imprint of Capstone
1710 Roe Crest Drive, North Mankato, Minnesota 56003
capstonepub.com

Library of Congress Cataloging-in-Publication Data is available on the Library of Congress website.
ISBN: 9781669076278 (hardcover)
ISBN: 9781669076223 (paperback)
ISBN: 9781669076230 (ebook PDF)

Summary: Playful graphics and text take readers on a historical tour of the United States congress and how people are elected to the Senate or House of Representatives, including lesser-known inside information.

Editorial Credits
Editor: Mandy Robbins; Designer: Heidi Thompson; Production Specialist: Tori Abraham

CONTENTS

INTRODUCTION: NEW TO CAPITOL HILL

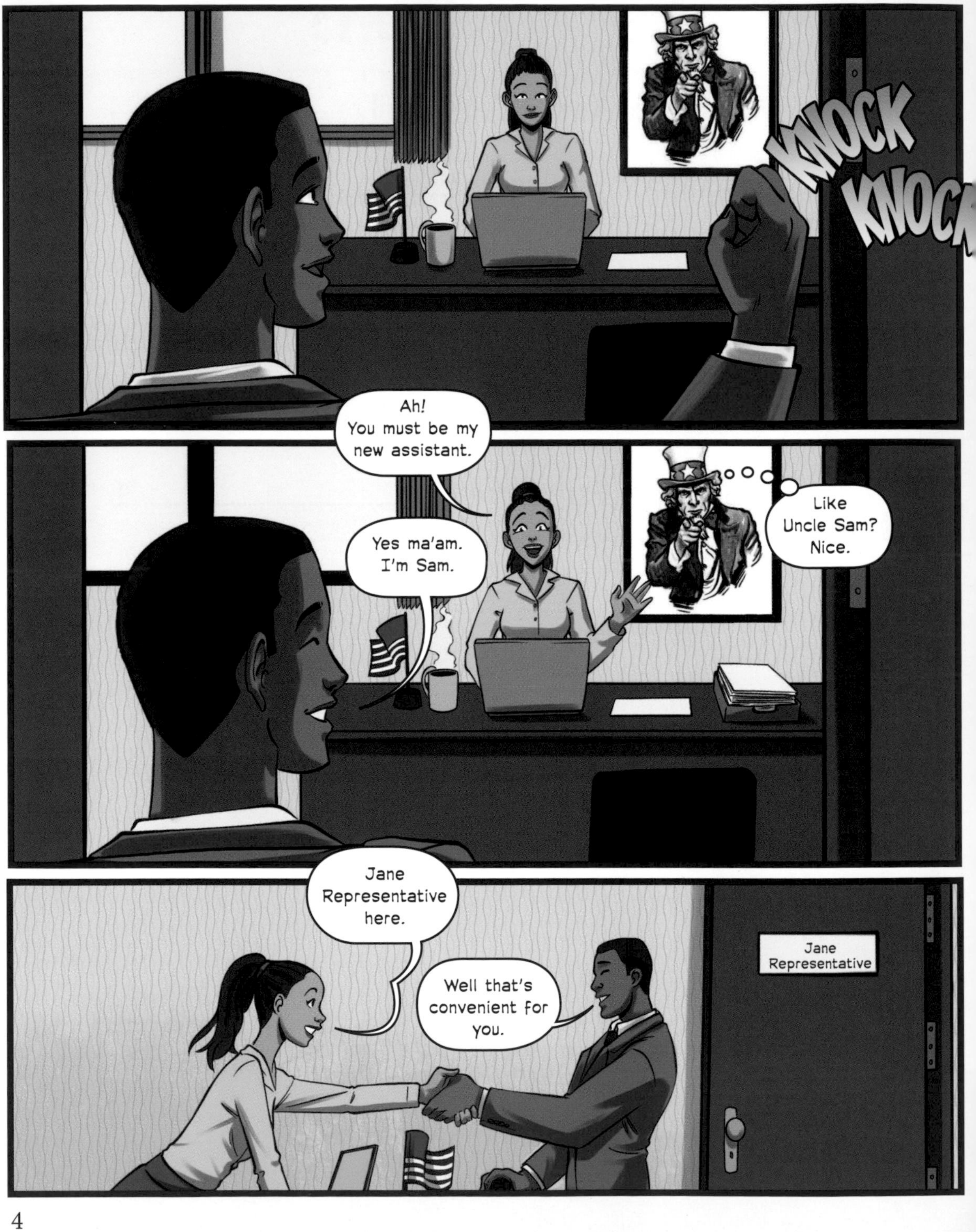

KNOCK KNOCK
Ah! You must be my new assistant.
Yes ma'am. I'm Sam.
Like Uncle Sam? Nice.
Jane Representative here.
Well that's convenient for you.
Jane Representative

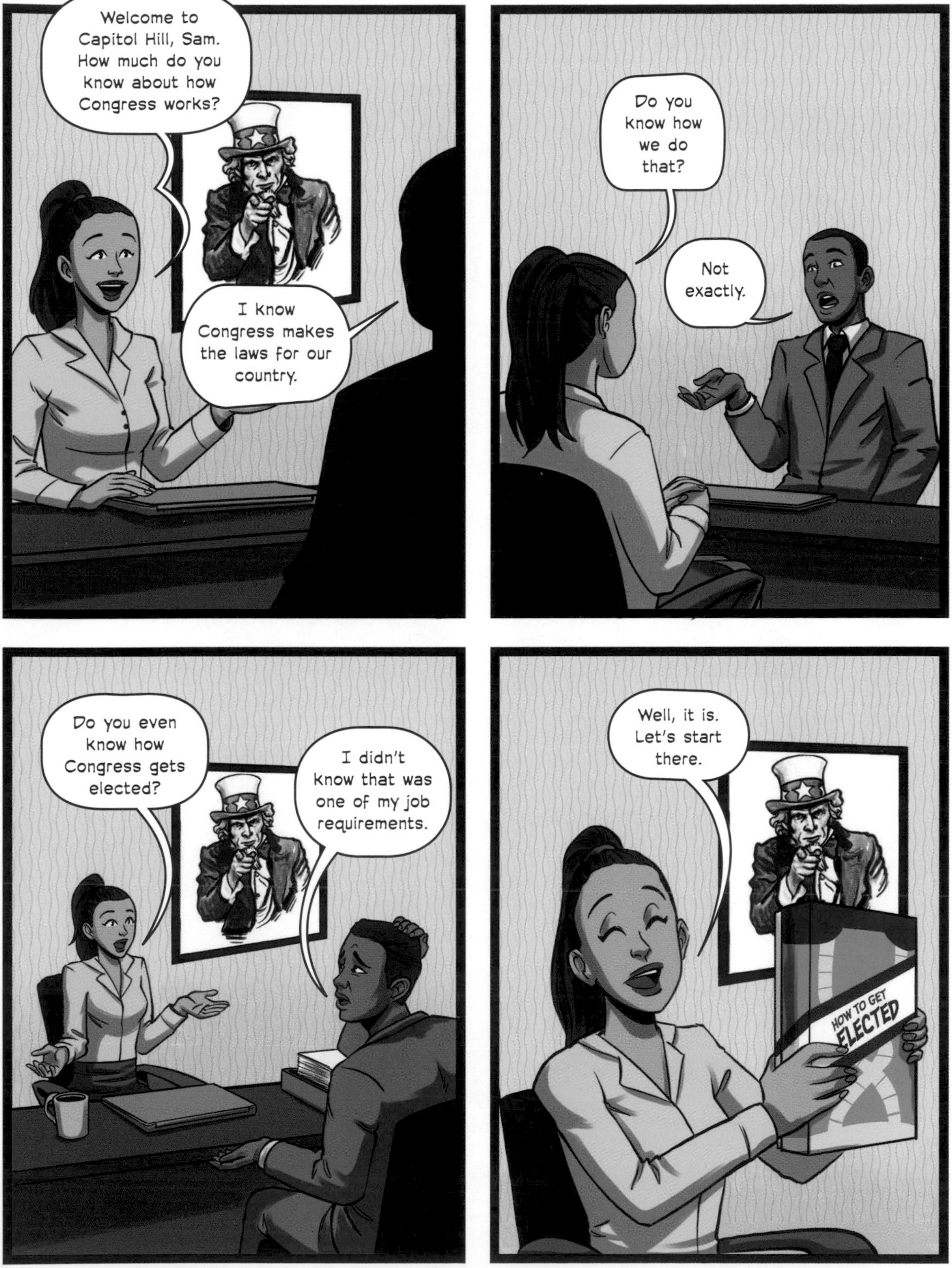
Welcome to Capitol Hill, Sam. How much do you know about how Congress works?
I know Congress makes the laws for our country.
Do you know how we do that?
Not exactly.
Do you even know how Congress gets elected?
I didn't know that was one of my job requirements.
Well, it is. Let's start there.
HOW TO GET ELECTED

CHAPTER ONE: GETTING ELECTED

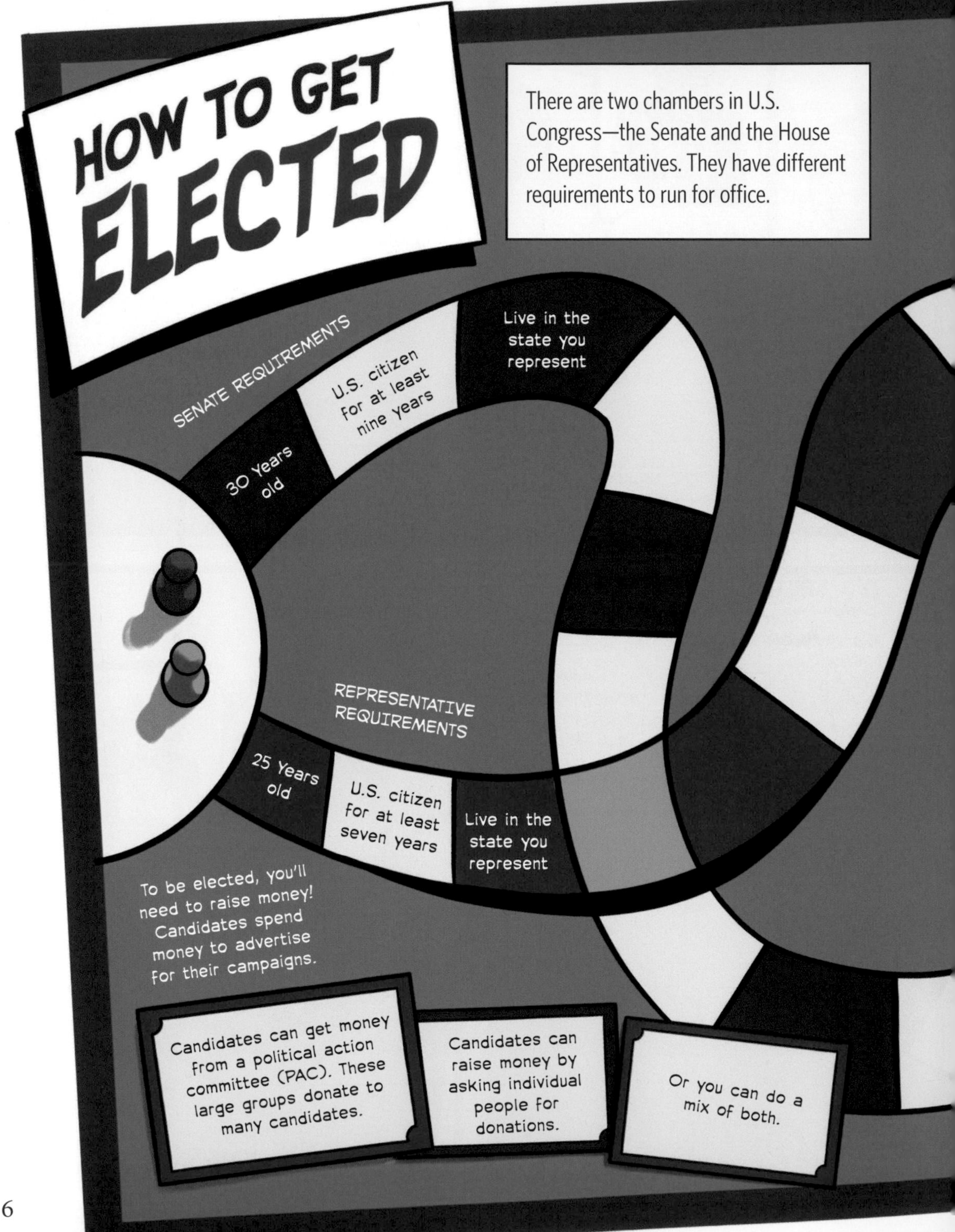
HOW TO GET ELECTED
There are two chambers in U.S. Congress—the Senate and the House of Representatives. They have different requirements to run for office.
SENATE REQUIREMENTS
30 Years old
U.S. citizen for at least nine years
Live in the state you represent
REPRESENTATIVE REQUIREMENTS
25 Years old
U.S. citizen for at least seven years
Live in the state you represent
To be elected, you'll need to raise money! Candidates spend money to advertise for their campaigns.
Candidates can get money from a political action committee (PAC). These large groups donate to many candidates.
Candidates can raise money by asking individual people for donations.
Or you can do a mix of both.

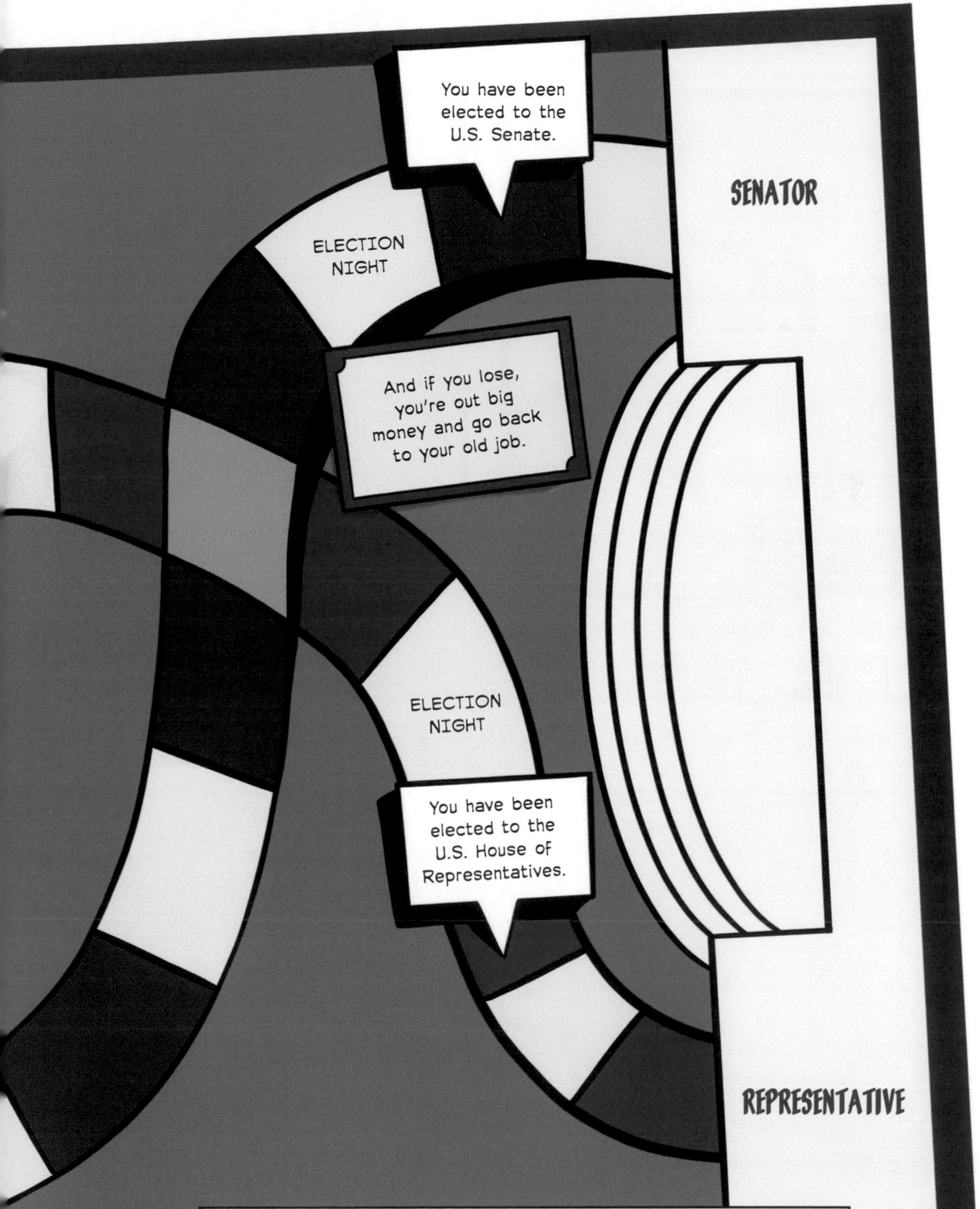
You have been elected to the U.S. Senate.
SENATOR
ELECTION NIGHT
And if you lose, you're out big money and go back to your old job.
ELECTION NIGHT
You have been elected to the U.S. House of Representatives.
REPRESENTATIVE

FACT!

Senators are elected to six-year terms. Representatives are elected to two-year terms. There's no limit on how many times someone can be elected to Congress.

CHAPTER TWO: THE CONSTITUTIONAL CONVERSATION

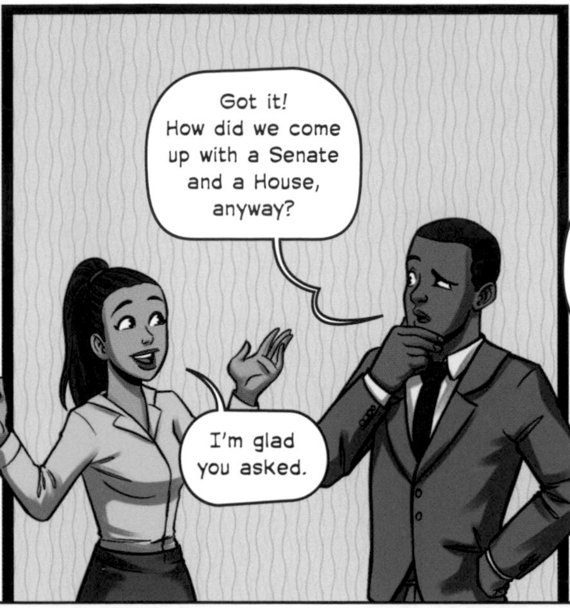

Got it! How did we come up with a Senate and a House, anyway?
I'm glad you asked.

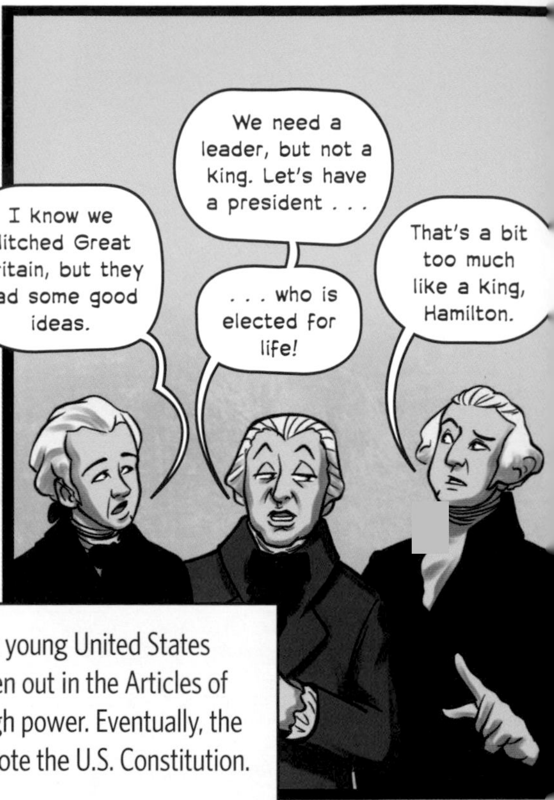

I know we ditched Great Britain, but they had some good ideas.
We need a leader, but not a king. Let's have a president . . .
. . . who is elected for life!
That's a bit too much like a king, Hamilton.

Picture it: The Philadelphia State House, 1787. Delegates of the young United States have met to improve their system of government. It was written out in the Articles of Confederation, but it didn't give the federal government enough power. Eventually, the delegates scrapped it and formed a new government. They wrote the U.S. Constitution.

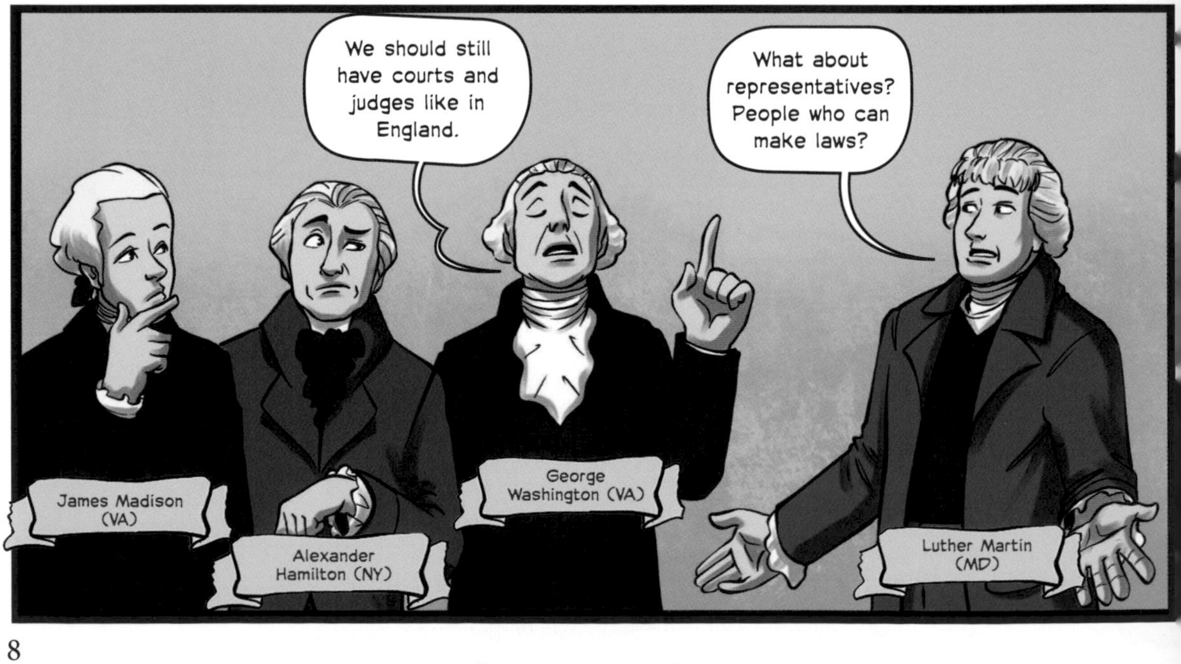

We should still have courts and judges like in England.
What about representatives? People who can make laws?
James Madison (VA)
Alexander Hamilton (NY)
George Washington (VA)
Luther Martin (MD)

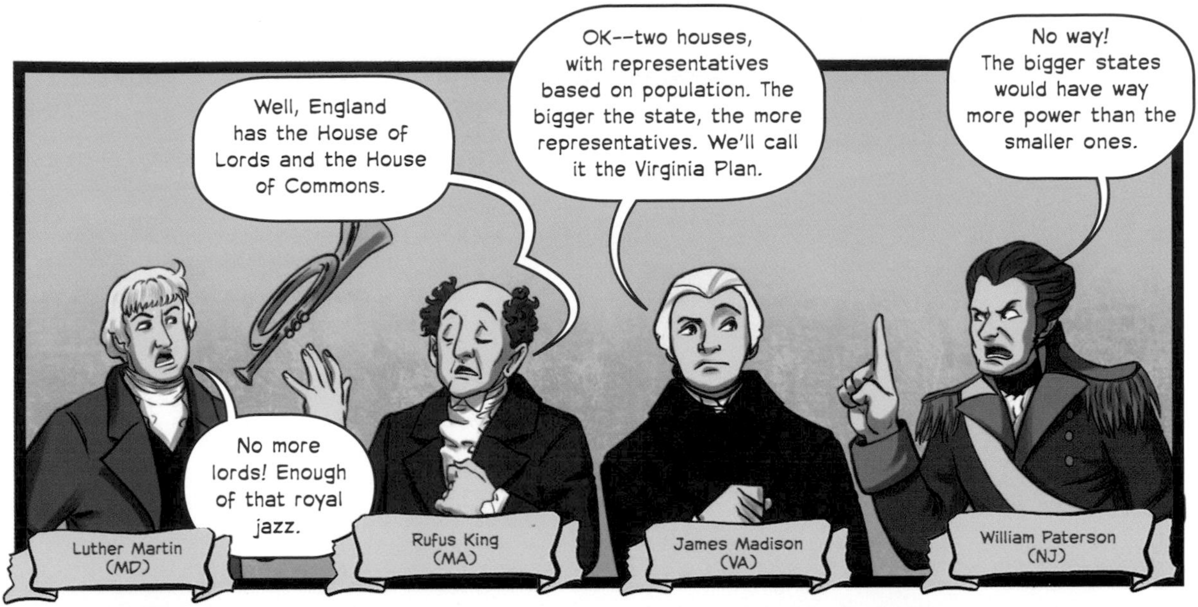
Well, England has the House of Lords and the House of Commons.
OK--two houses, with representatives based on population. The bigger the state, the more representatives. We'll call it the Virginia Plan.
No way! The bigger states would have way more power than the smaller ones.
No more lords! Enough of that royal jazz.
Luther Martin (MD)
Rufus King (MA)
James Madison (VA)
William Paterson (NJ)

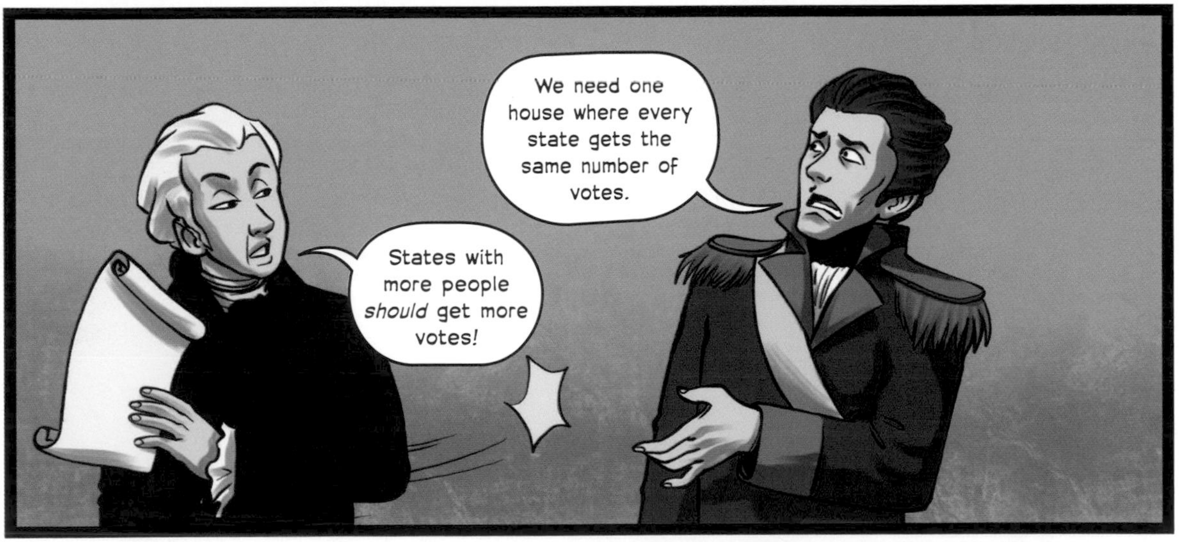
We need one house where every state gets the same number of votes.
States with more people *should* get more votes!

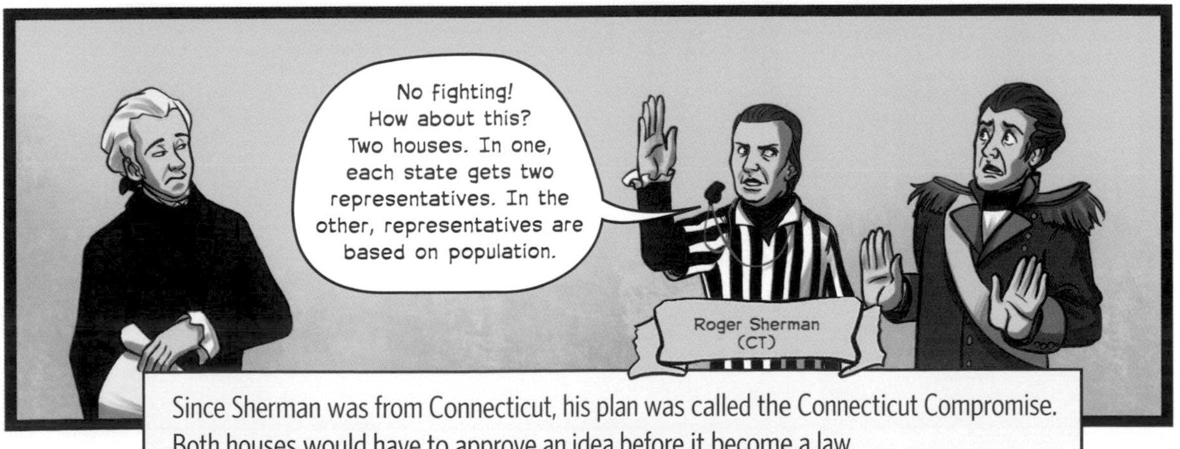
No fighting! How about this? Two houses. In one, each state gets two representatives. In the other, representatives are based on population.
Roger Sherman (CT)

Since Sherman was from Connecticut, his plan was called the Connecticut Compromise. Both houses would have to approve an idea before it become a law.

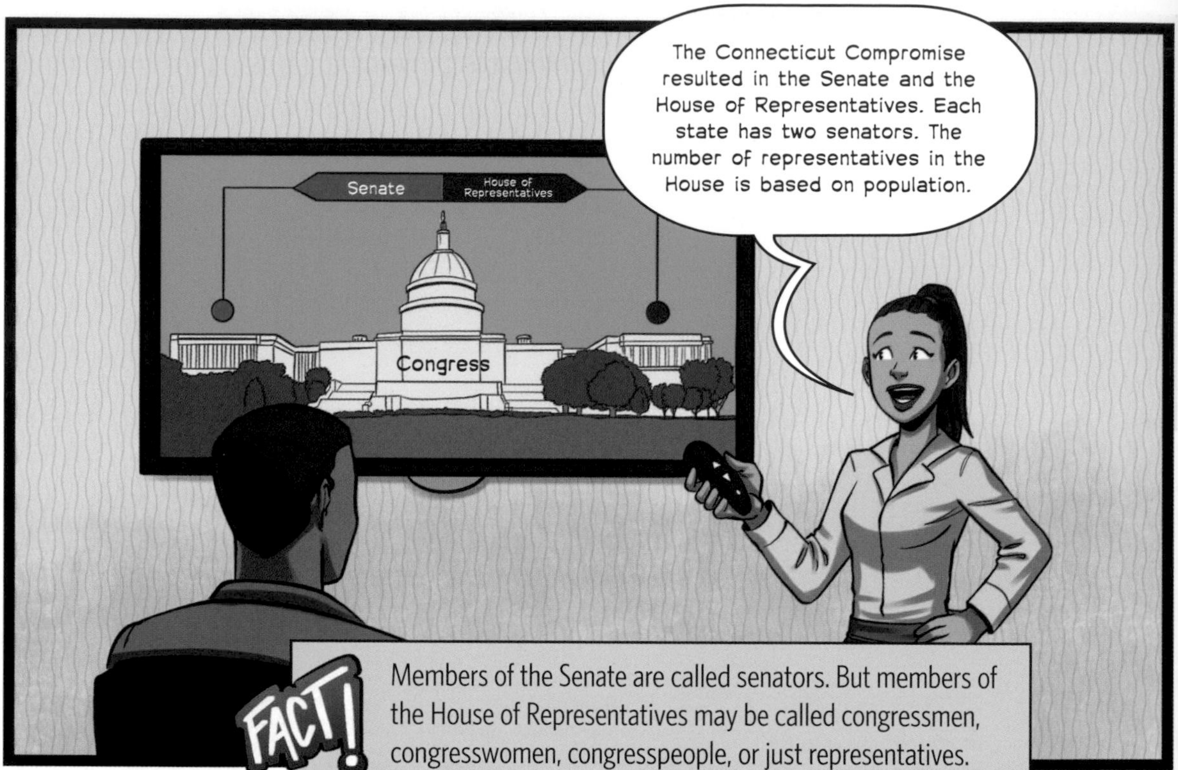
Senate
House of Representatives
Congress
The Connecticut Compromise resulted in the Senate and the House of Representatives. Each state has two senators. The number of representatives in the House is based on population.

FACT! Members of the Senate are called senators. But members of the House of Representatives may be called congressmen, congresswomen, congresspeople, or just representatives.

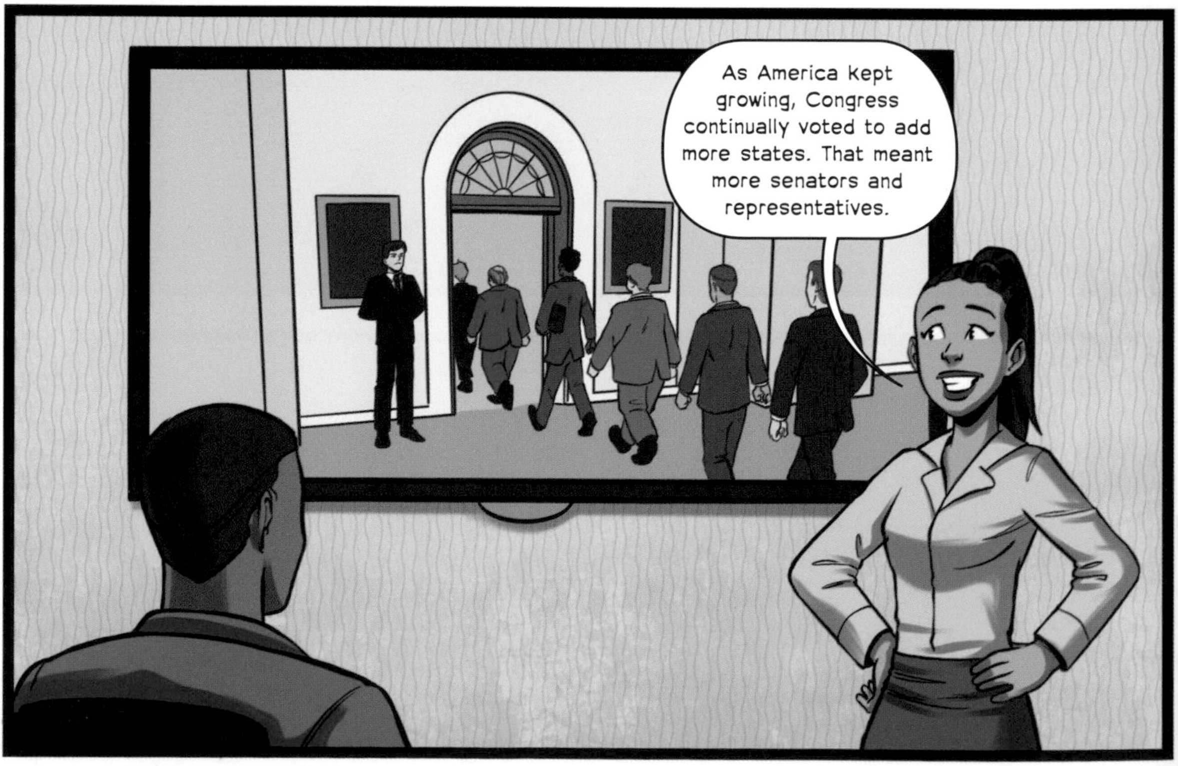
As America kept growing, Congress continually voted to add more states. That meant more senators and representatives.

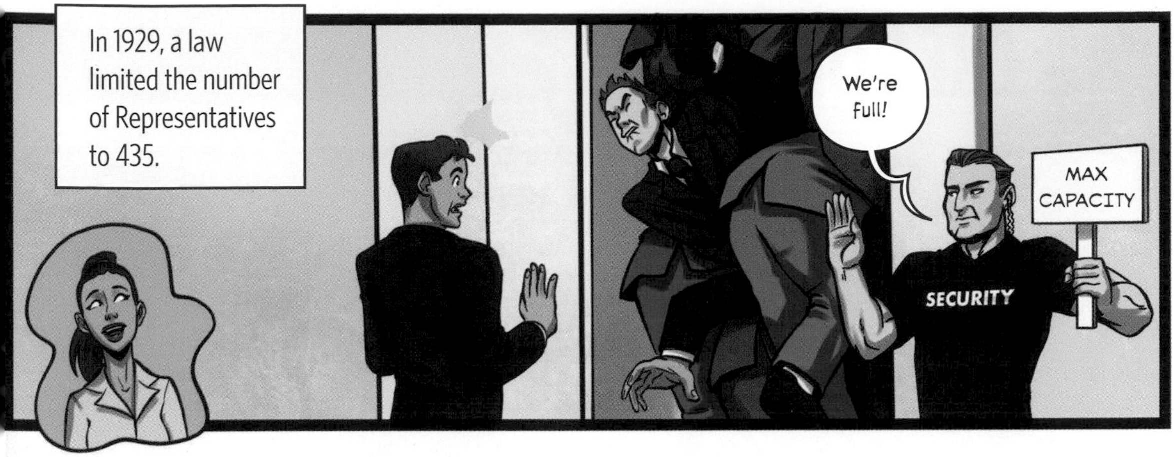
In 1929, a law limited the number of Representatives to 435.
We're full!
MAX CAPACITY
SECURITY

COUNT 'EM UP!

Every 10 years, the United States conducts a census. The government counts how many people are in the entire country. Based on those numbers, the states get different numbers of representatives. The state with the largest population, California, currently has 52 representatives. Six states—Alaska, Delaware, North Dakota, South Dakota, Vermont, and Wyoming—have only one representative each!

Now, those 435 Representatives are divided up among all 50 states!

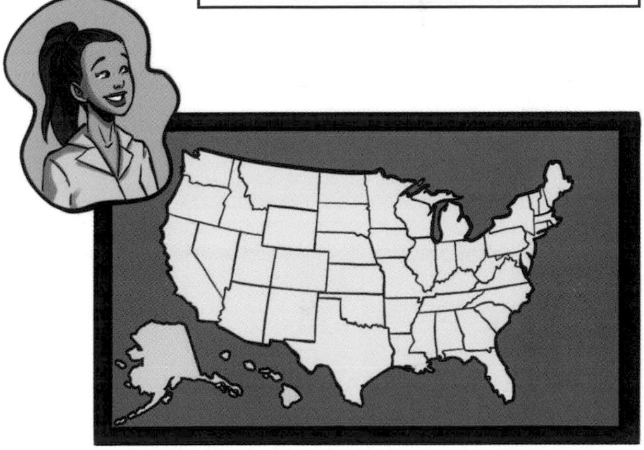

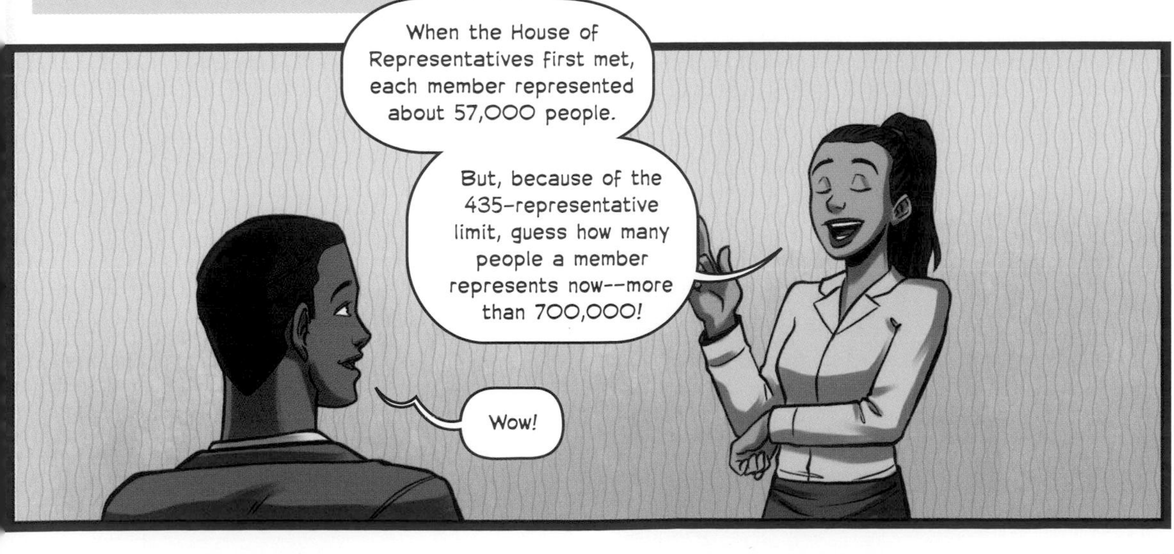
When the House of Representatives first met, each member represented about 57,000 people.
But, because of the 435-representative limit, guess how many people a member represents now--more than 700,000!
Wow!

CHAPTER THREE: CREATING LAWS

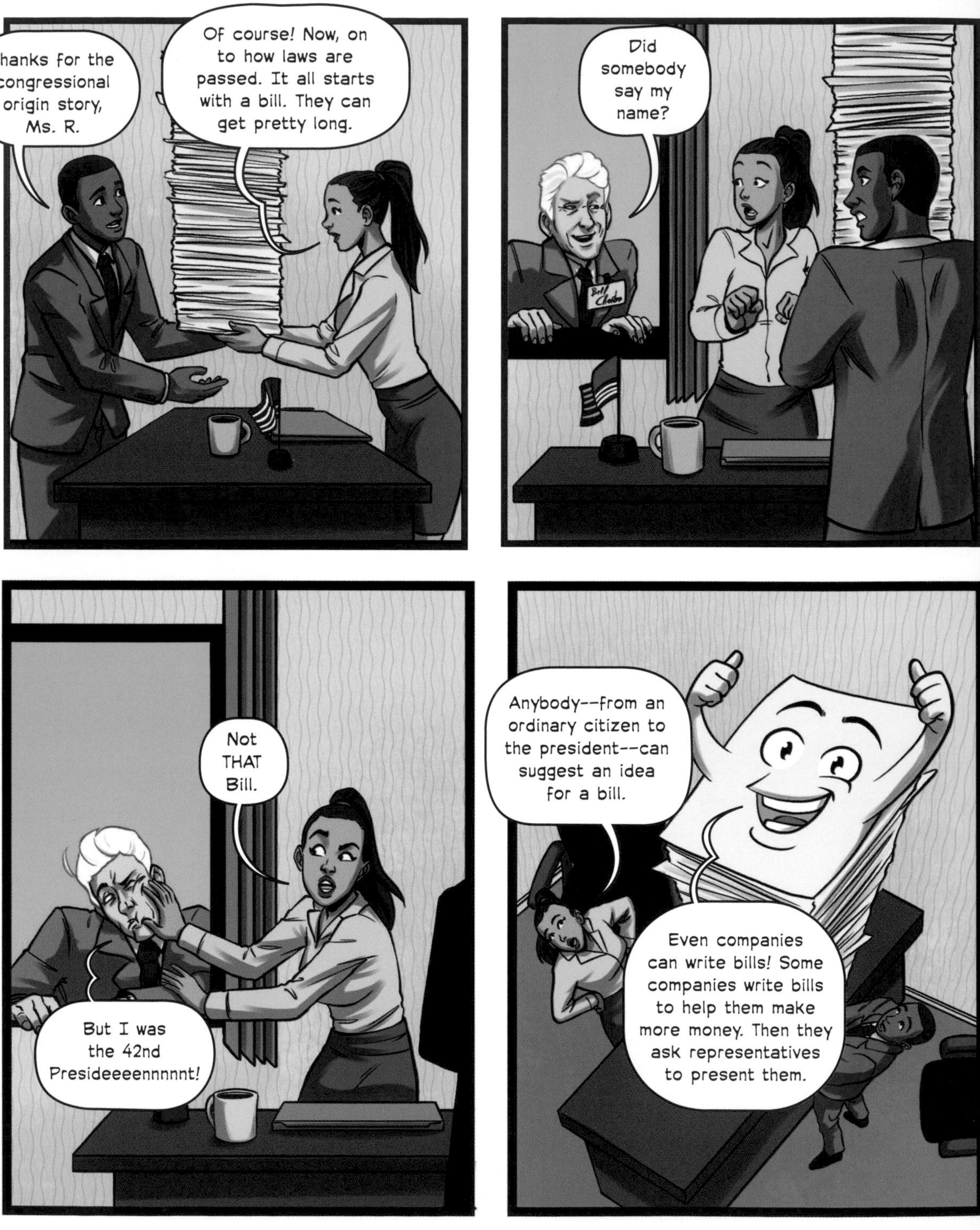
Thanks for the congressional origin story, Ms. R.
Of course! Now, on to how laws are passed. It all starts with a bill. They can get pretty long.
Did somebody say my name?
Not THAT Bill.
But I was the 42nd Presideeeennnnnt!
Anybody--from an ordinary citizen to the president--can suggest an idea for a bill.
Even companies can write bills! Some companies write bills to help them make more money. Then they ask representatives to present them.

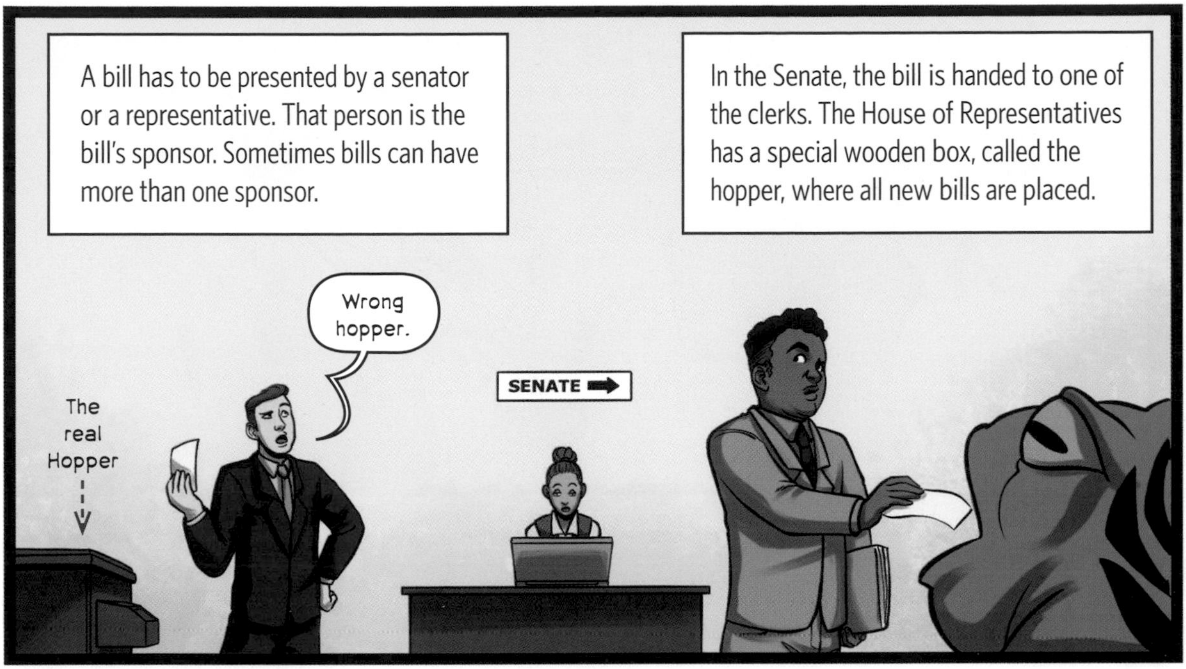
A bill has to be presented by a senator or a representative. That person is the bill's sponsor. Sometimes bills can have more than one sponsor.
In the Senate, the bill is handed to one of the clerks. The House of Representatives has a special wooden box, called the hopper, where all new bills are placed.
The real Hopper
Wrong hopper.
SENATE

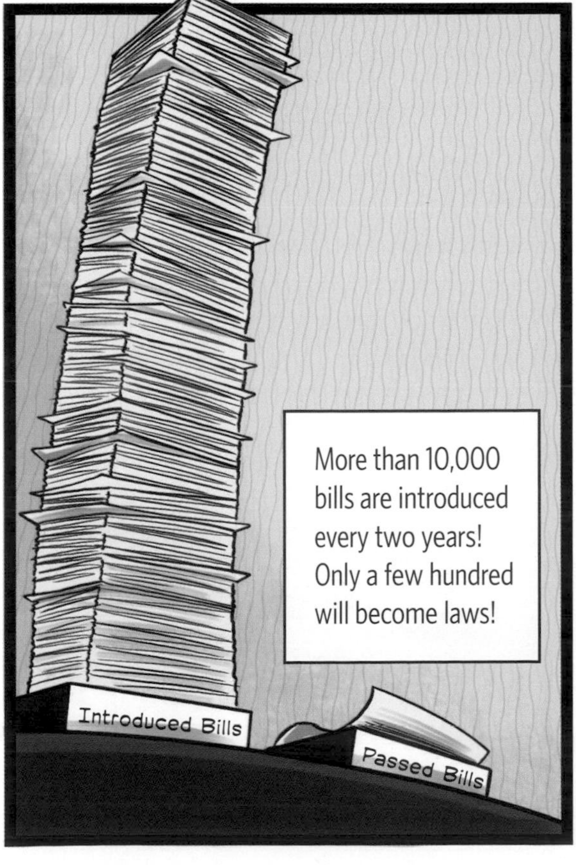
More than 10,000 bills are introduced every two years! Only a few hundred will become laws!
Introduced Bills
Passed Bills

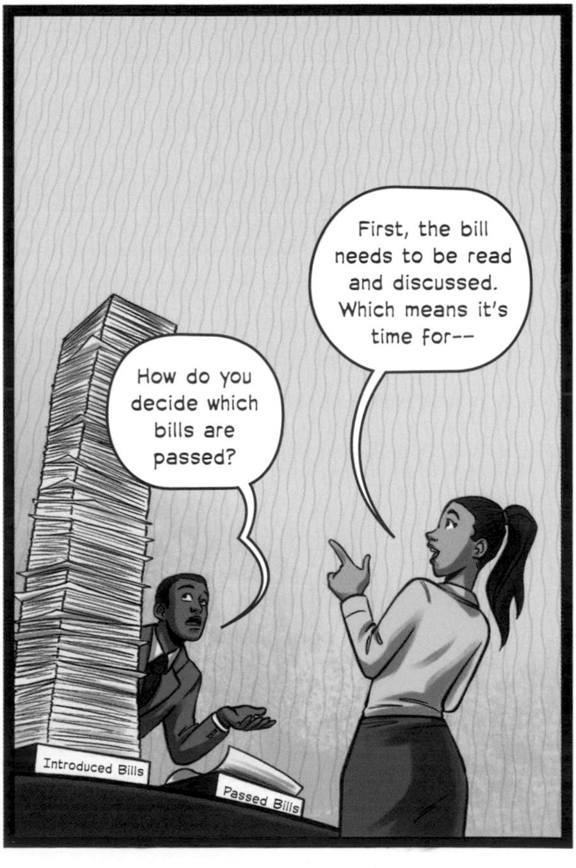
How do you decide which bills are passed?
First, the bill needs to be read and discussed. Which means it's time for--
Introduced Bills
Passed Bills

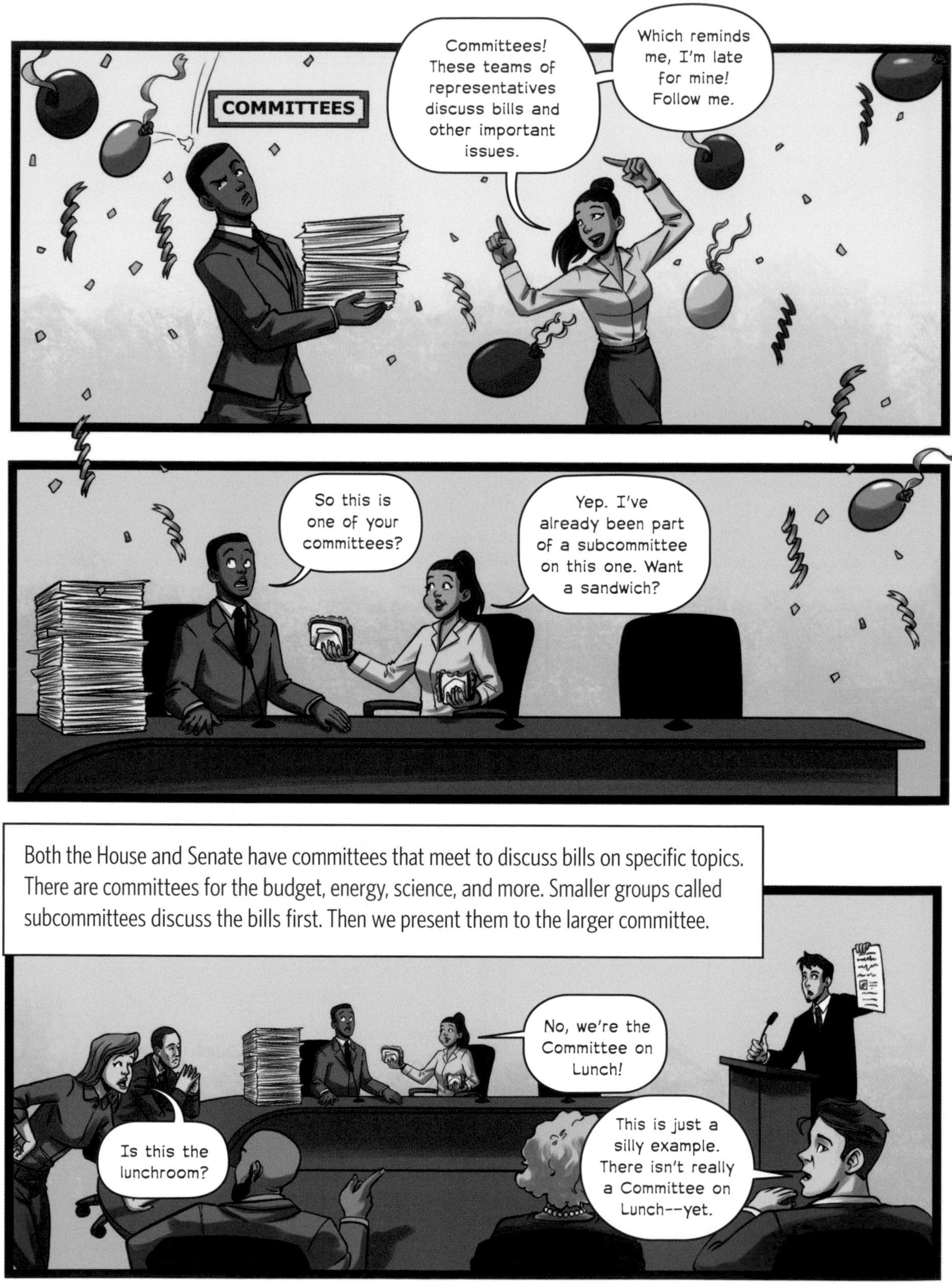
COMMITTEES
Committees! These teams of representatives discuss bills and other important issues.
Which reminds me, I'm late for mine! Follow me.
So this is one of your committees?
Yep. I've already been part of a subcommittee on this one. Want a sandwich?
Both the House and Senate have committees that meet to discuss bills on specific topics. There are committees for the budget, energy, science, and more. Smaller groups called subcommittees discuss the bills first. Then we present them to the larger committee.
Is this the lunchroom?
No, we're the Committee on Lunch!
This is just a silly example. There isn't really a Committee on Lunch--yet.

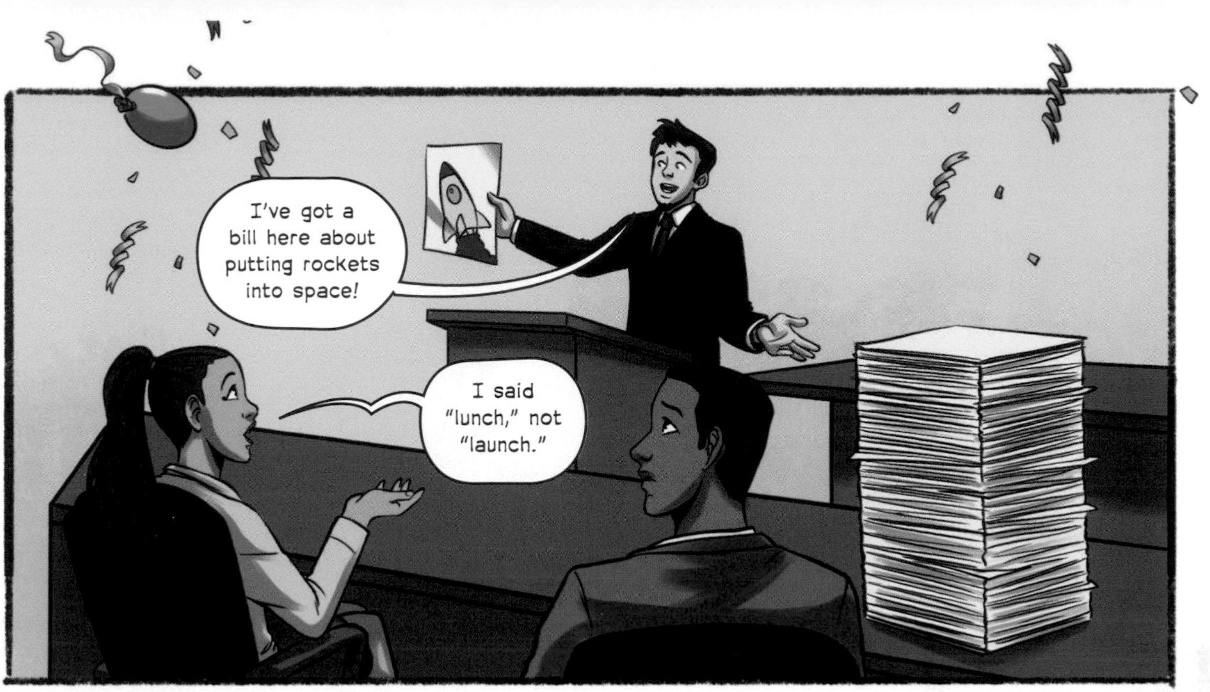
I've got a bill here about putting rockets into space!
I said "lunch," not "launch."

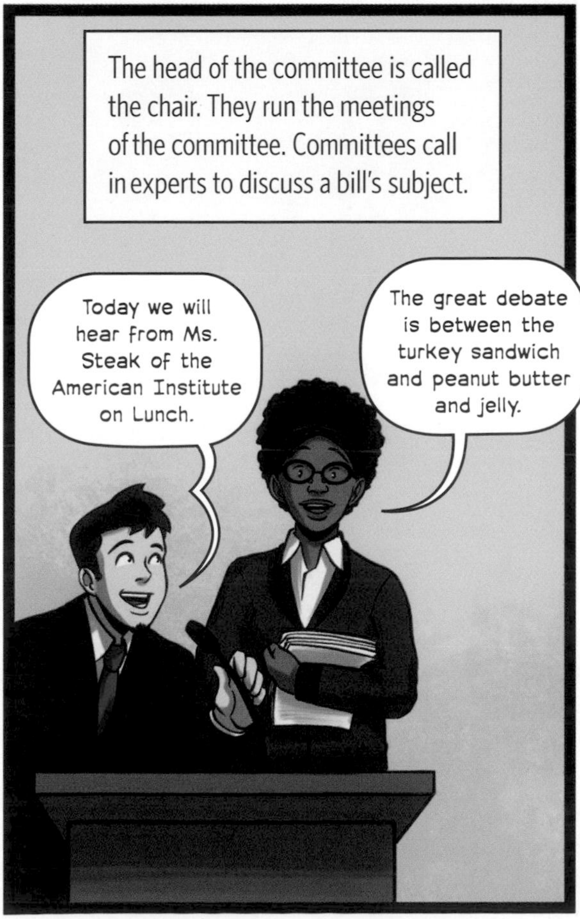
The head of the committee is called the chair. They run the meetings of the committee. Committees call in experts to discuss a bill's subject.
Today we will hear from Ms. Steak of the American Institute on Lunch.
The great debate is between the turkey sandwich and peanut butter and jelly.

COMMITTEES AND COMIC BOOKS

Sometimes, special committees are formed to investigate current events. In 1953, the Senate created the Subcommittee to Investigate Juvenile Delinquency. At the time, comic books were hugely popular with kids, especially books about crime and horror.

Adults were worried these books would have a negative effect on children. Members of the committee discussed whether certain types of comic books were turning children into criminals. In the end, the First Amendment's protection of the freedom of the press won out, and kids got to keep their comic books.

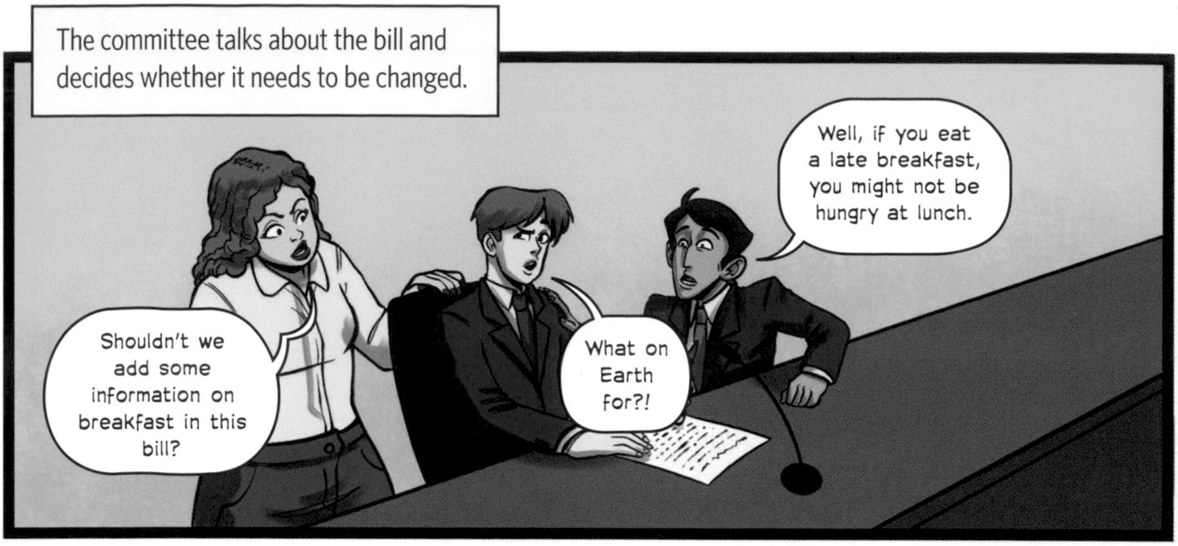
The committee talks about the bill and decides whether it needs to be changed.
Shouldn't we add some information on breakfast in this bill?
What on Earth for?!
Well, if you eat a late breakfast, you might not be hungry at lunch.

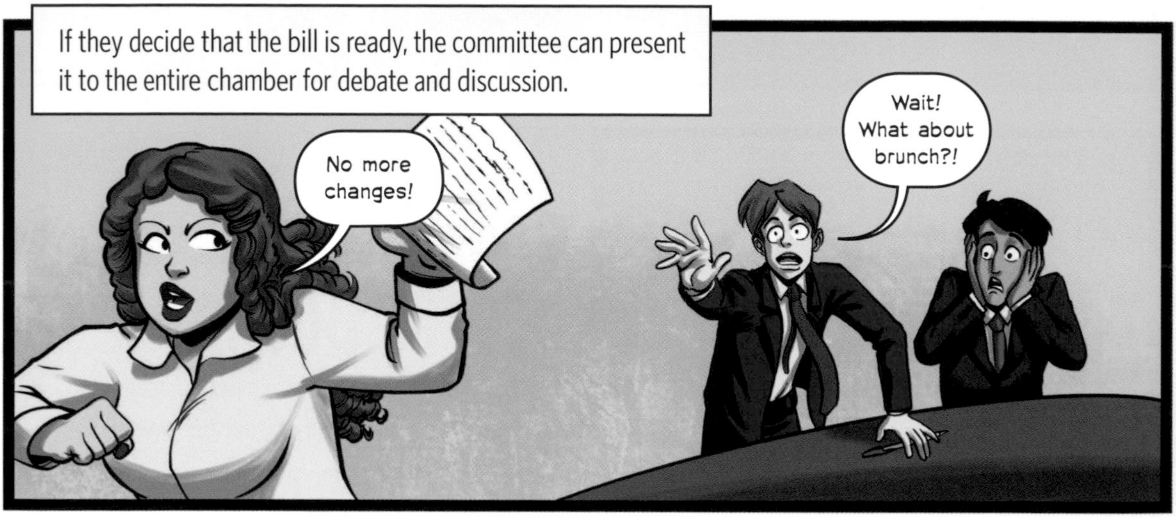
If they decide that the bill is ready, the committee can present it to the entire chamber for debate and discussion.
No more changes!
Wait! What about brunch?!

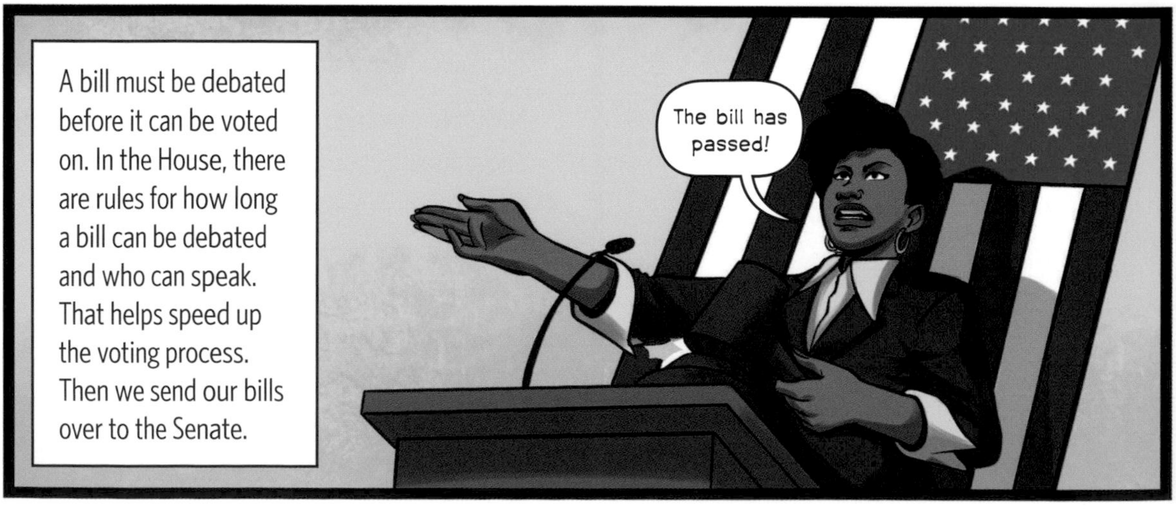
A bill must be debated before it can be voted on. In the House, there are rules for how long a bill can be debated and who can speak. That helps speed up the voting process. Then we send our bills over to the Senate.
The bill has passed!

The Senate has fewer rules. Senators can debate a bill as long as they want. If a senator really doesn't want a bill to pass, they will speak for a super long time. That's called a filibuster.

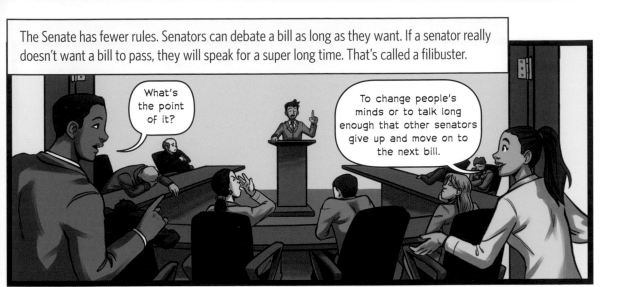

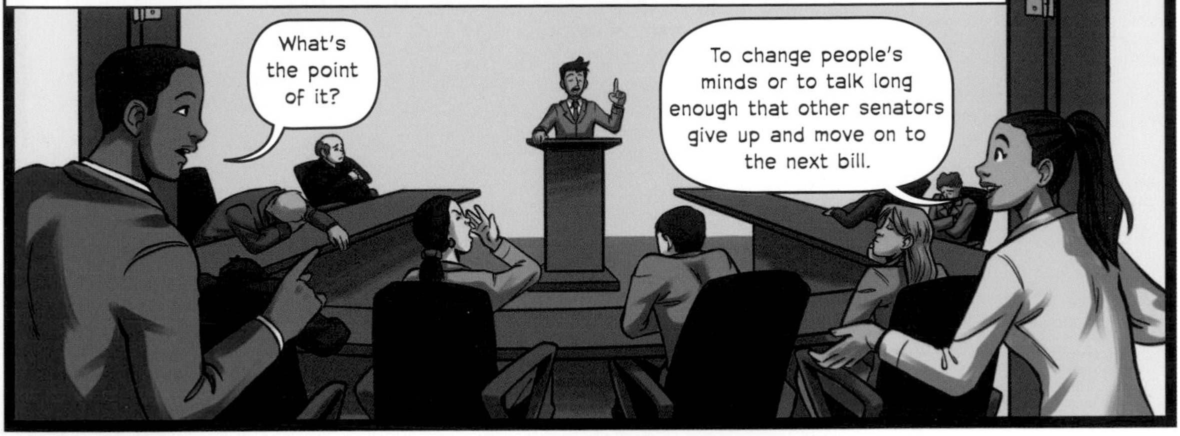
What's the point of it?
To change people's minds or to talk long enough that other senators give up and move on to the next bill.

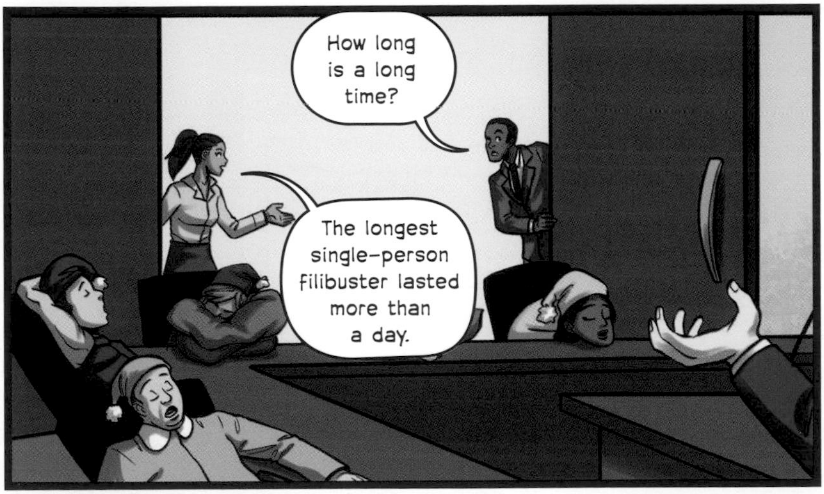
How long is a long time?
The longest single-person filibuster lasted more than a day.

FACT!

In 1957, South Carolina Senator Strom Thurmond spoke for 24 hours and 18 minutes to protest a civil rights bill.

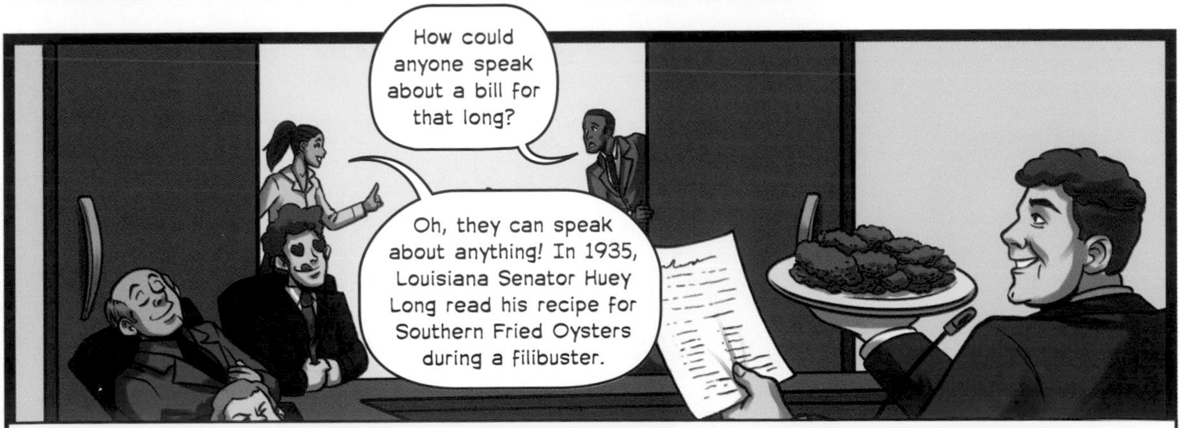
How could anyone speak about a bill for that long?
Oh, they can speak about anything! In 1935, Louisiana Senator Huey Long read his recipe for Southern Fried Oysters during a filibuster.

The only way to end a filibuster and force a vote is for 60 senators to vote in favor of ending the debate. These days, it's pretty impossible to get 60 senators to agree on anything.

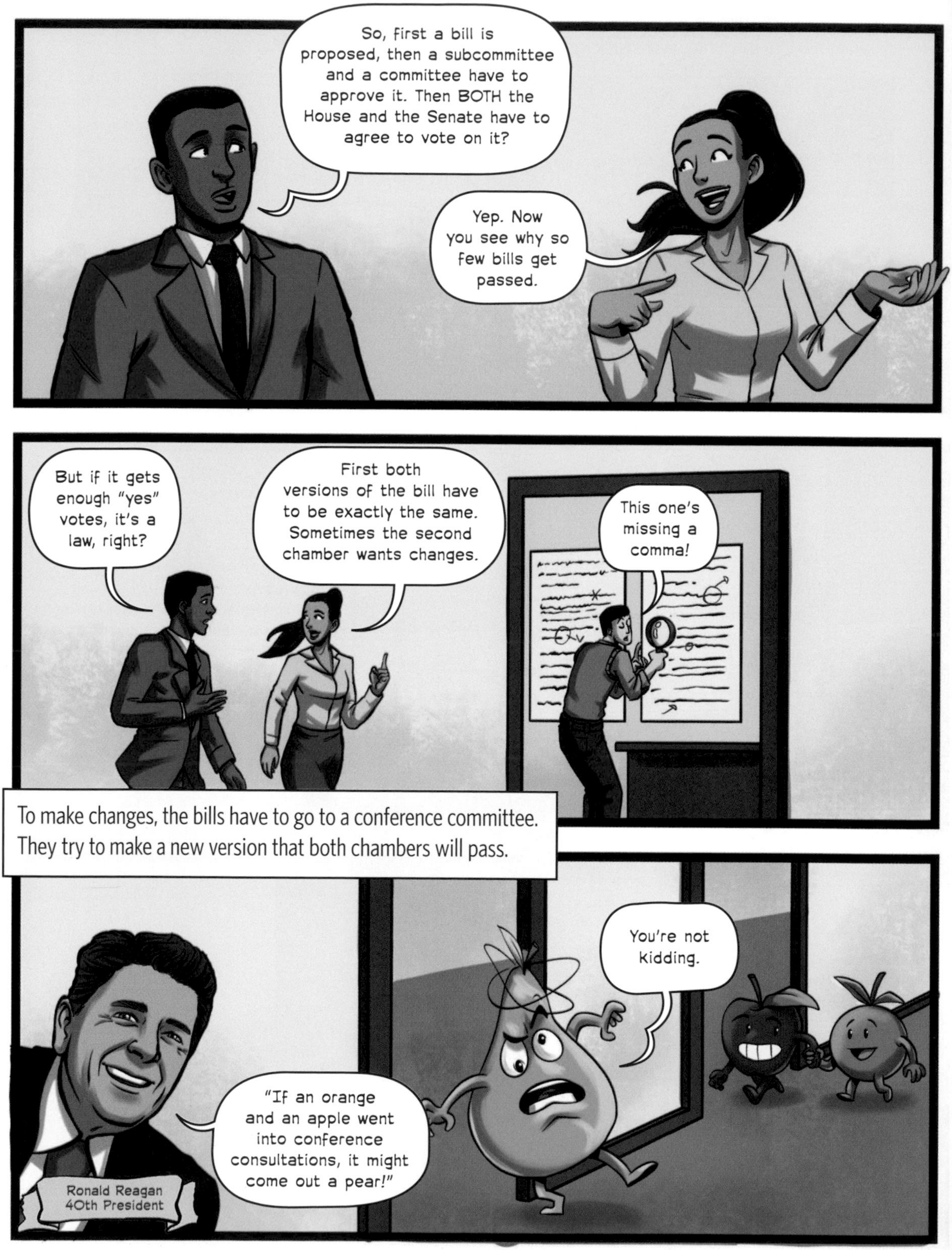
So, first a bill is proposed, then a subcommittee and a committee have to approve it. Then BOTH the House and the Senate have to agree to vote on it?
Yep. Now you see why so few bills get passed.
But if it gets enough "yes" votes, it's a law, right?
First both versions of the bill have to be exactly the same. Sometimes the second chamber wants changes.
This one's missing a comma!
To make changes, the bills have to go to a conference committee. They try to make a new version that both chambers will pass.
Ronald Reagan
40th President
"If an orange and an apple went into conference consultations, it might come out a pear!"
You're not kidding.

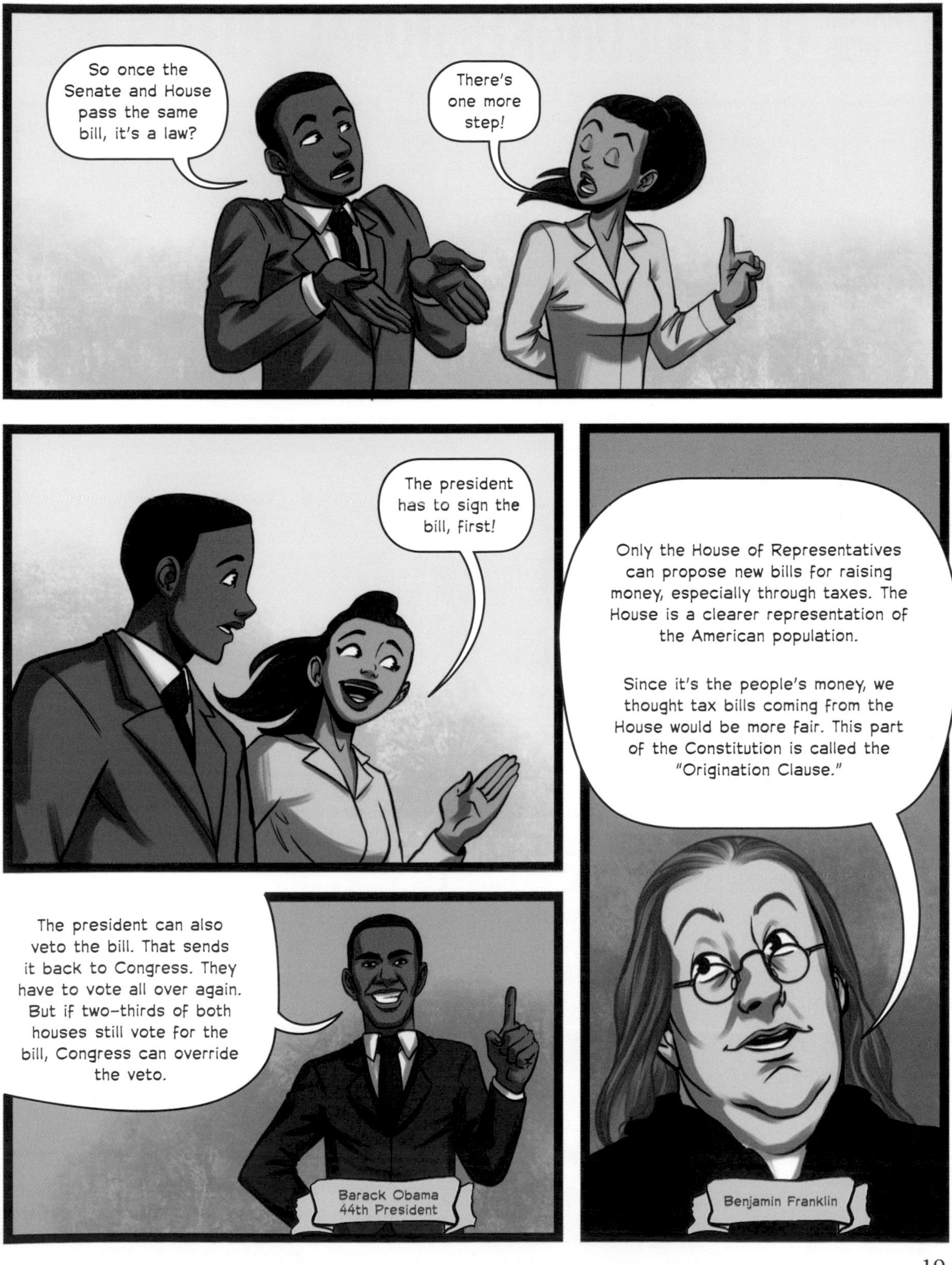
So once the Senate and House pass the same bill, it's a law?
There's one more step!
The president has to sign the bill, first!
Only the House of Representatives can propose new bills for raising money, especially through taxes. The House is a clearer representation of the American population.
Since it's the people's money, we thought tax bills coming from the House would be more fair. This part of the Constitution is called the "Origination Clause."
Benjamin Franklin
The president can also veto the bill. That sends it back to Congress. They have to vote all over again. But if two-thirds of both houses still vote for the bill, Congress can override the veto.
Barack Obama
44th President

CHAPTER FOUR: OTHER CONGRESSIONAL DUTIES

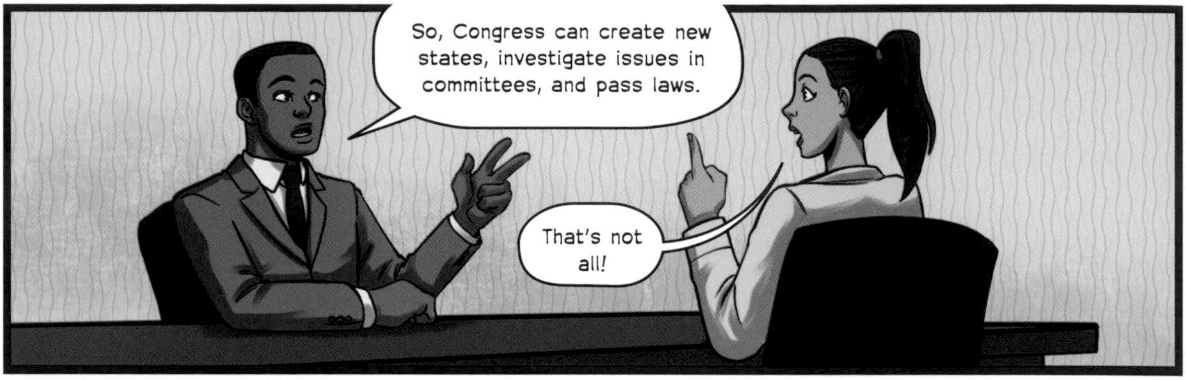
So, Congress can create new states, investigate issues in committees, and pass laws.
That's not all!

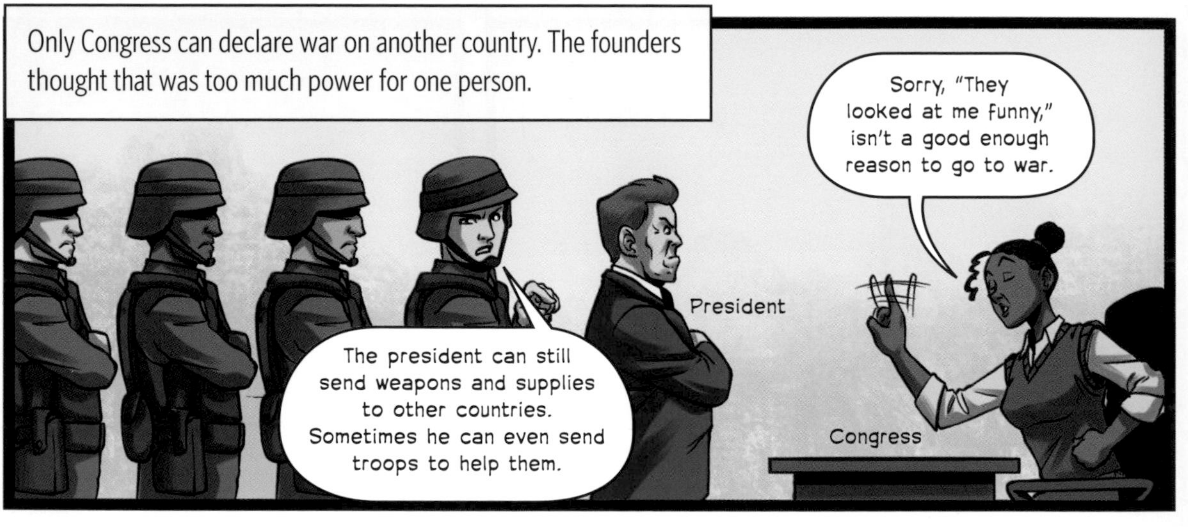
Only Congress can declare war on another country. The founders thought that was too much power for one person.
Sorry, "They looked at me funny," isn't a good enough reason to go to war.
President
Congress
The president can still send weapons and supplies to other countries. Sometimes he can even send troops to help them.

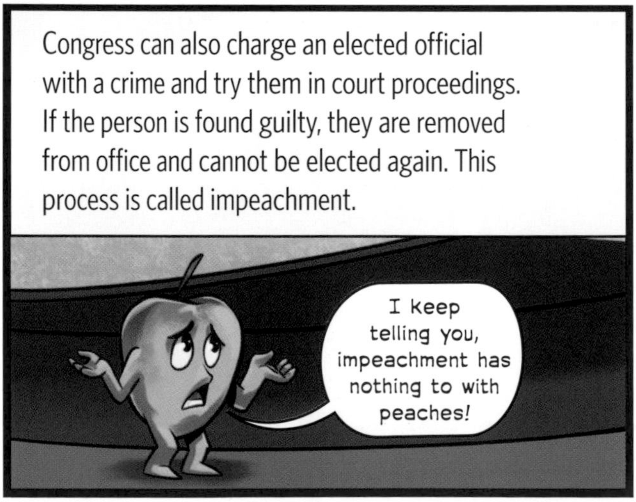
Congress can also charge an elected official with a crime and try them in court proceedings. If the person is found guilty, they are removed from office and cannot be elected again. This process is called impeachment.
I keep telling you, impeachment has nothing to with peaches!

IMPEACHMENT

Each chamber of Congress has different powers when it comes to impeachment. Only the House can charge an official with a crime. Two-thirds of the representatives must agree in order for this to happen. Then the Senate serves as the court that tries the person.

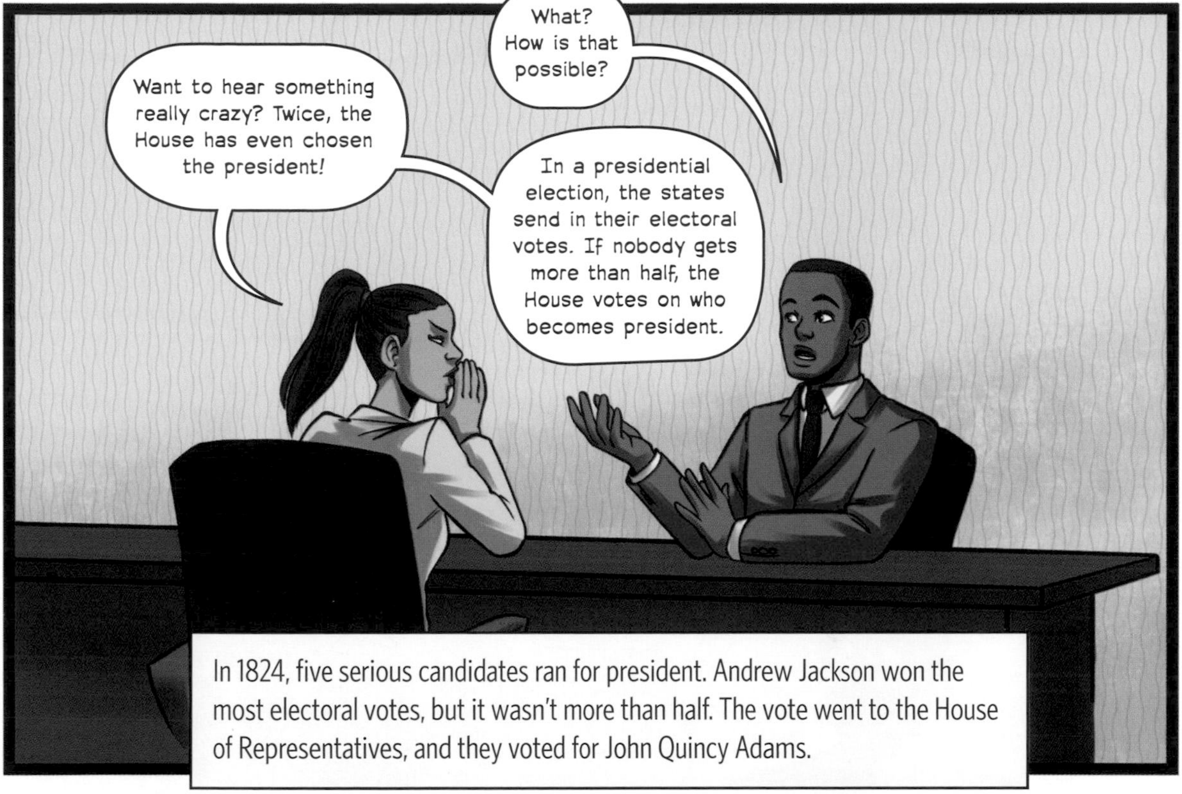
Want to hear something really crazy? Twice, the House has even chosen the president!
What? How is that possible?
In a presidential election, the states send in their electoral votes. If nobody gets more than half, the House votes on who becomes president.
In 1824, five serious candidates ran for president. Andrew Jackson won the most electoral votes, but it wasn't more than half. The vote went to the House of Representatives, and they voted for John Quincy Adams.

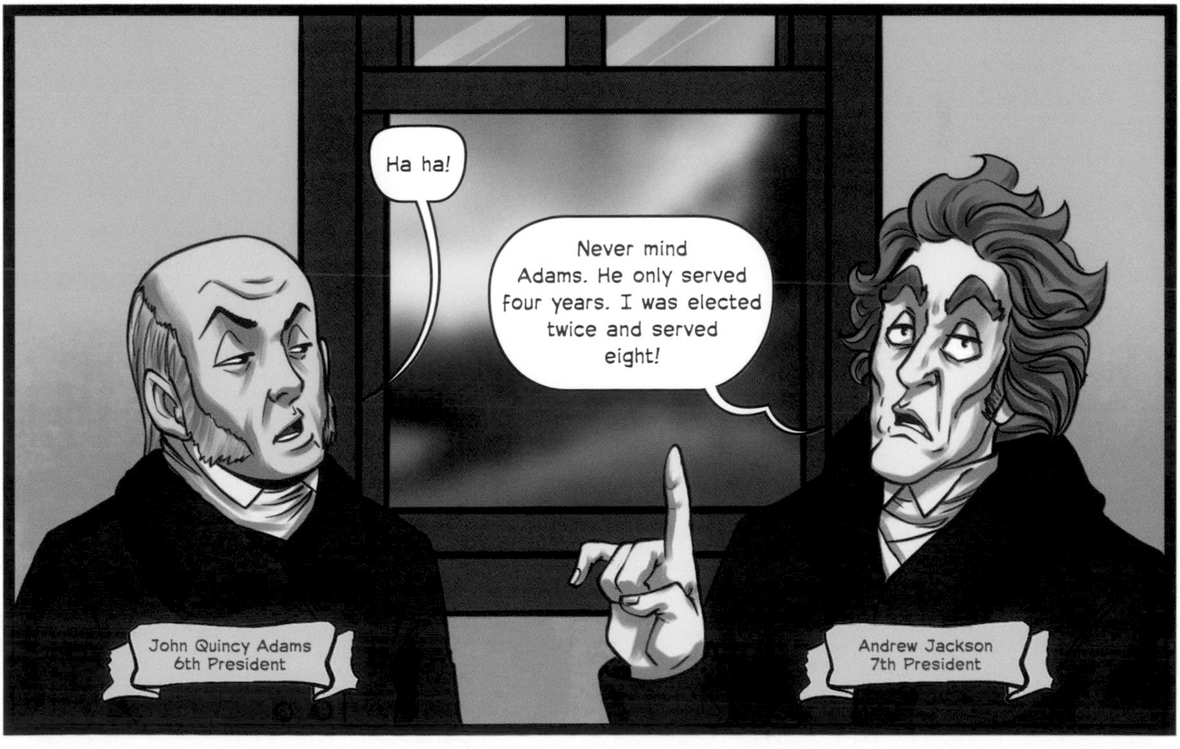
Ha ha!
Never mind Adams. He only served four years. I was elected twice and served eight!
John Quincy Adams 6th President
Andrew Jackson 7th President

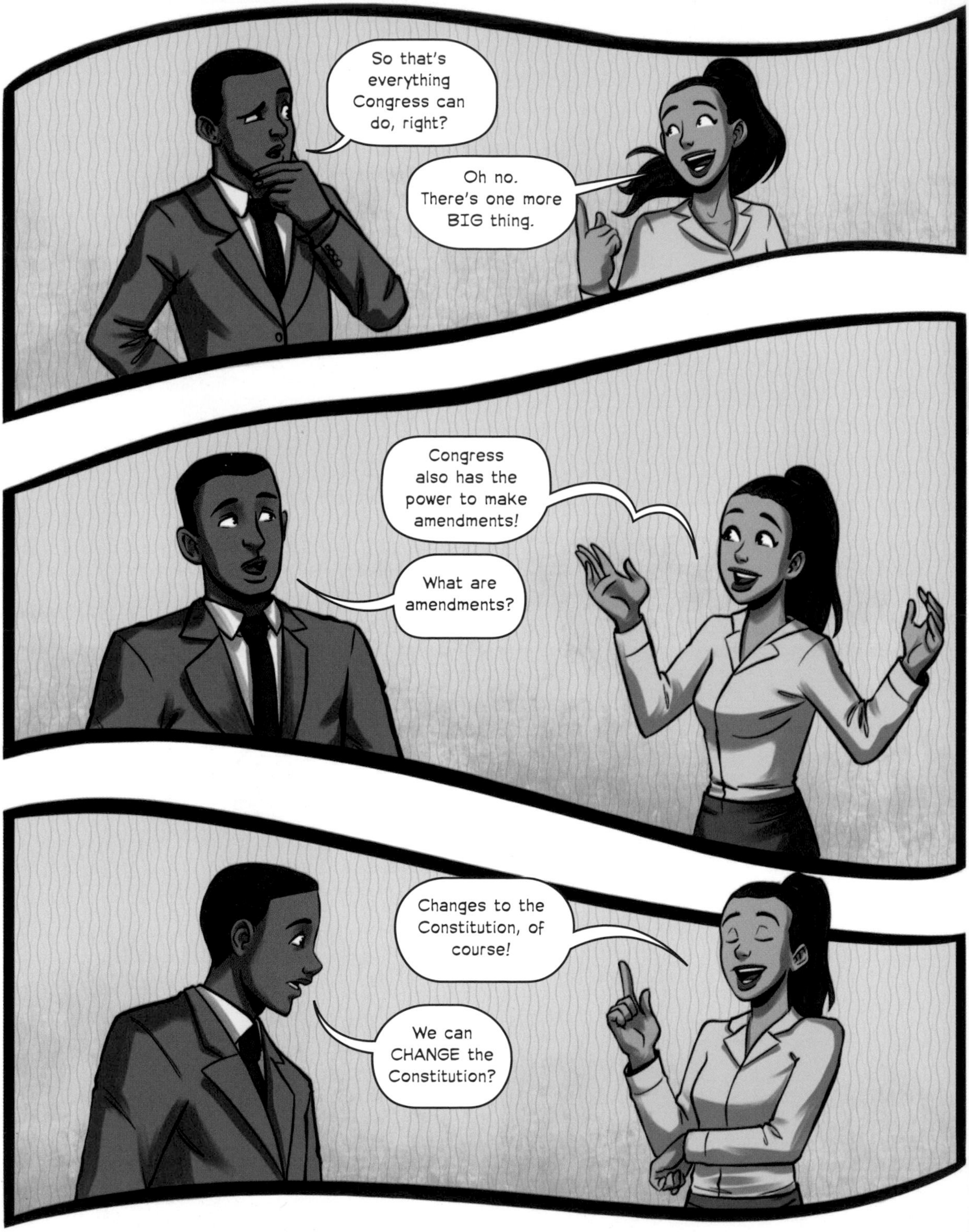
So that's everything Congress can do, right?
Oh no. There's one more BIG thing.
Congress also has the power to make amendments!
What are amendments?
Changes to the Constitution, of course!
We can CHANGE the Constitution?

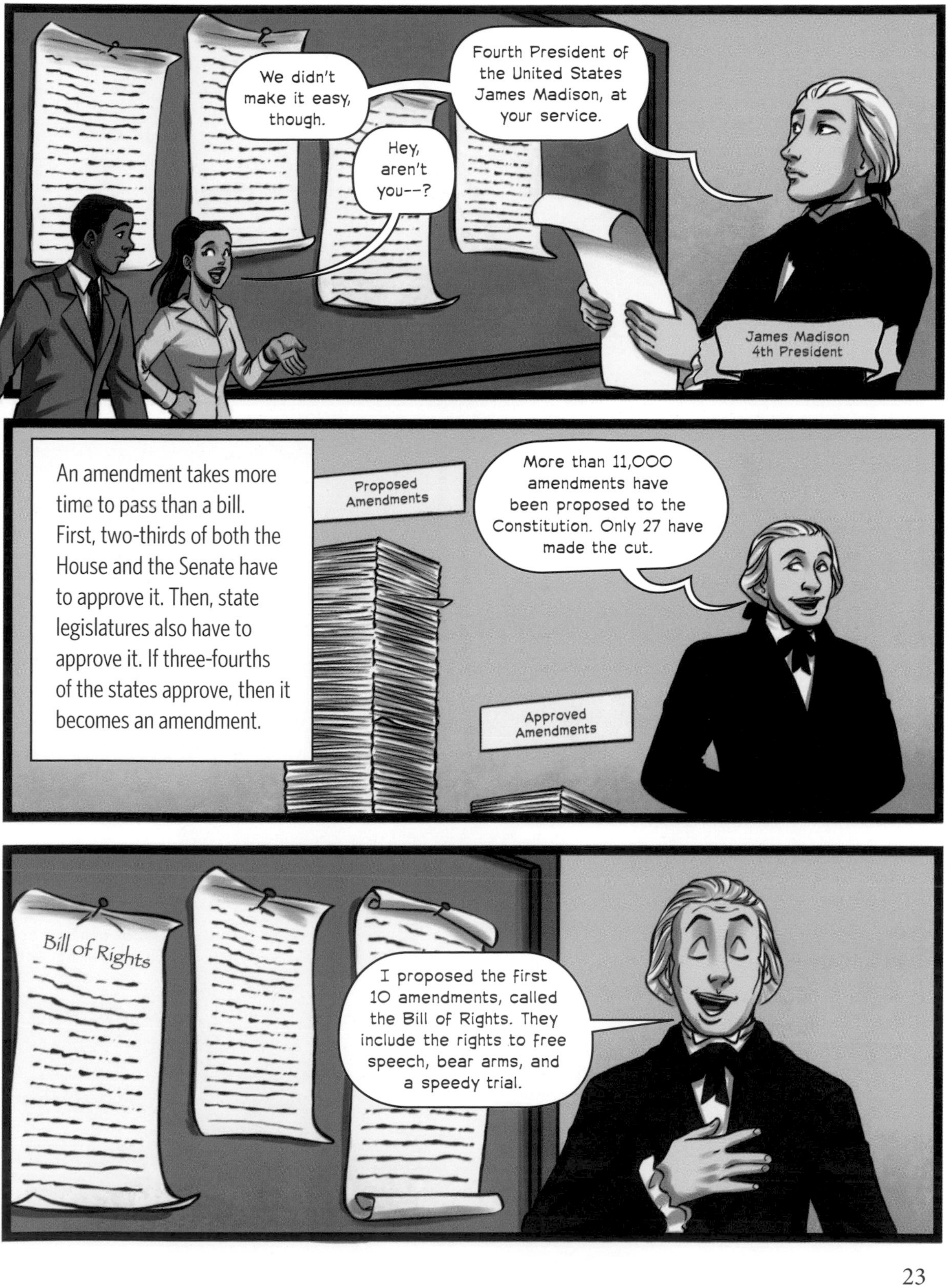
Hey, aren't you--?
Fourth President of the United States James Madison, at your service.
We didn't make it easy, though.
James Madison 4th President
An amendment takes more time to pass than a bill. First, two-thirds of both the House and the Senate have to approve it. Then, state legislatures also have to approve it. If three-fourths of the states approve, then it becomes an amendment.
Proposed Amendments
More than 11,000 amendments have been proposed to the Constitution. Only 27 have made the cut.
Approved Amendments
Bill of Rights
I proposed the first 10 amendments, called the Bill of Rights. They include the rights to free speech, bear arms, and a speedy trial.

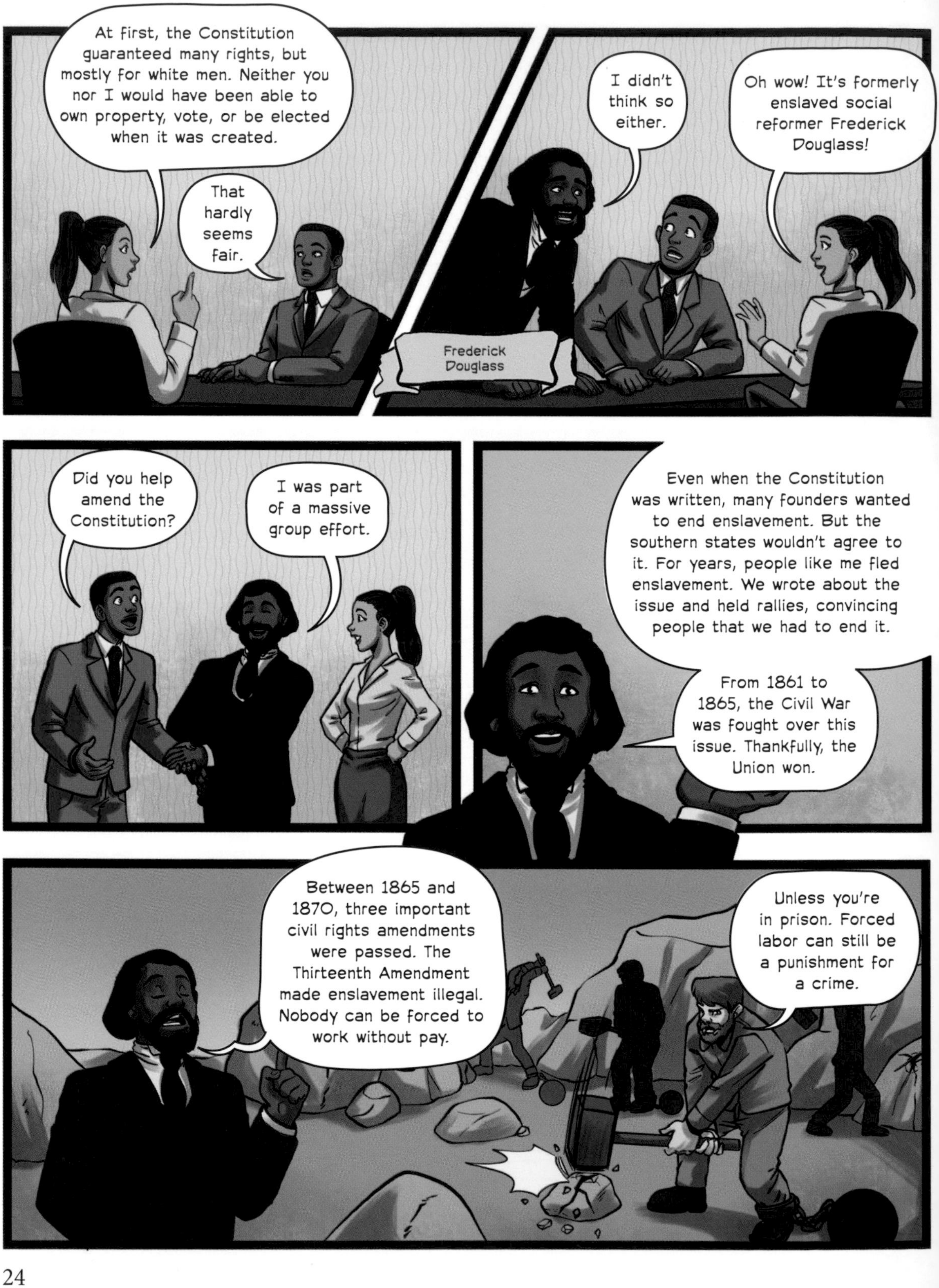

At first, the Constitution guaranteed many rights, but mostly for white men. Neither you nor I would have been able to own property, vote, or be elected when it was created.
That hardly seems fair.
I didn't think so either.
Oh wow! It's formerly enslaved social reformer Frederick Douglass!
Frederick Douglass
Did you help amend the Constitution?
I was part of a massive group effort.
Even when the Constitution was written, many founders wanted to end enslavement. But the southern states wouldn't agree to it. For years, people like me fled enslavement. We wrote about the issue and held rallies, convincing people that we had to end it.
From 1861 to 1865, the Civil War was fought over this issue. Thankfully, the Union won.
Between 1865 and 1870, three important civil rights amendments were passed. The Thirteenth Amendment made enslavement illegal. Nobody can be forced to work without pay.
Unless you're in prison. Forced labor can still be a punishment for a crime.

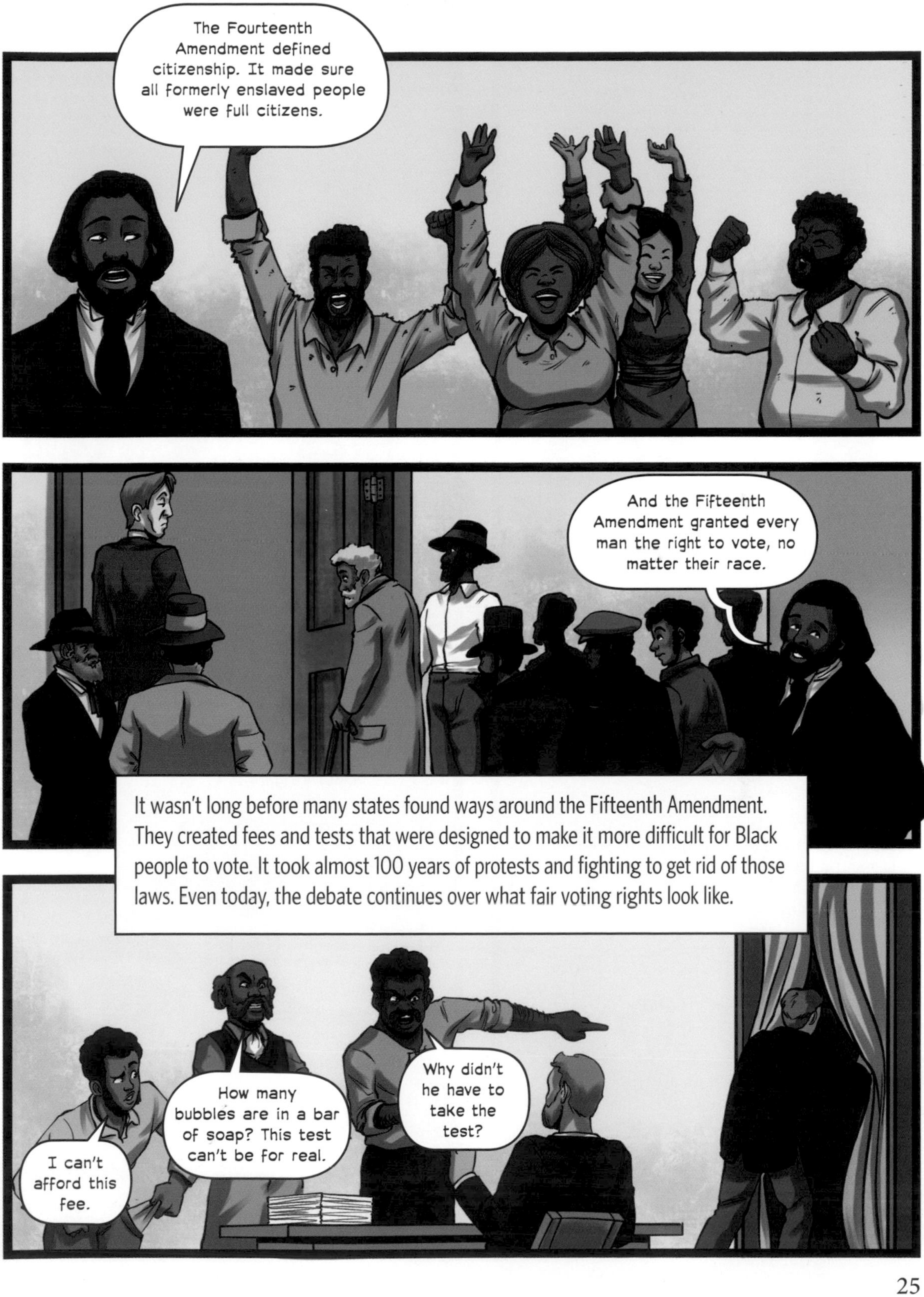
The Fourteenth Amendment defined citizenship. It made sure all formerly enslaved people were full citizens.
And the Fifteenth Amendment granted every man the right to vote, no matter their race.
It wasn't long before many states found ways around the Fifteenth Amendment. They created fees and tests that were designed to make it more difficult for Black people to vote. It took almost 100 years of protests and fighting to get rid of those laws. Even today, the debate continues over what fair voting rights look like.
I can't afford this fee.
How many bubbles are in a bar of soap? This test can't be for real.
Why didn't he have to take the test?

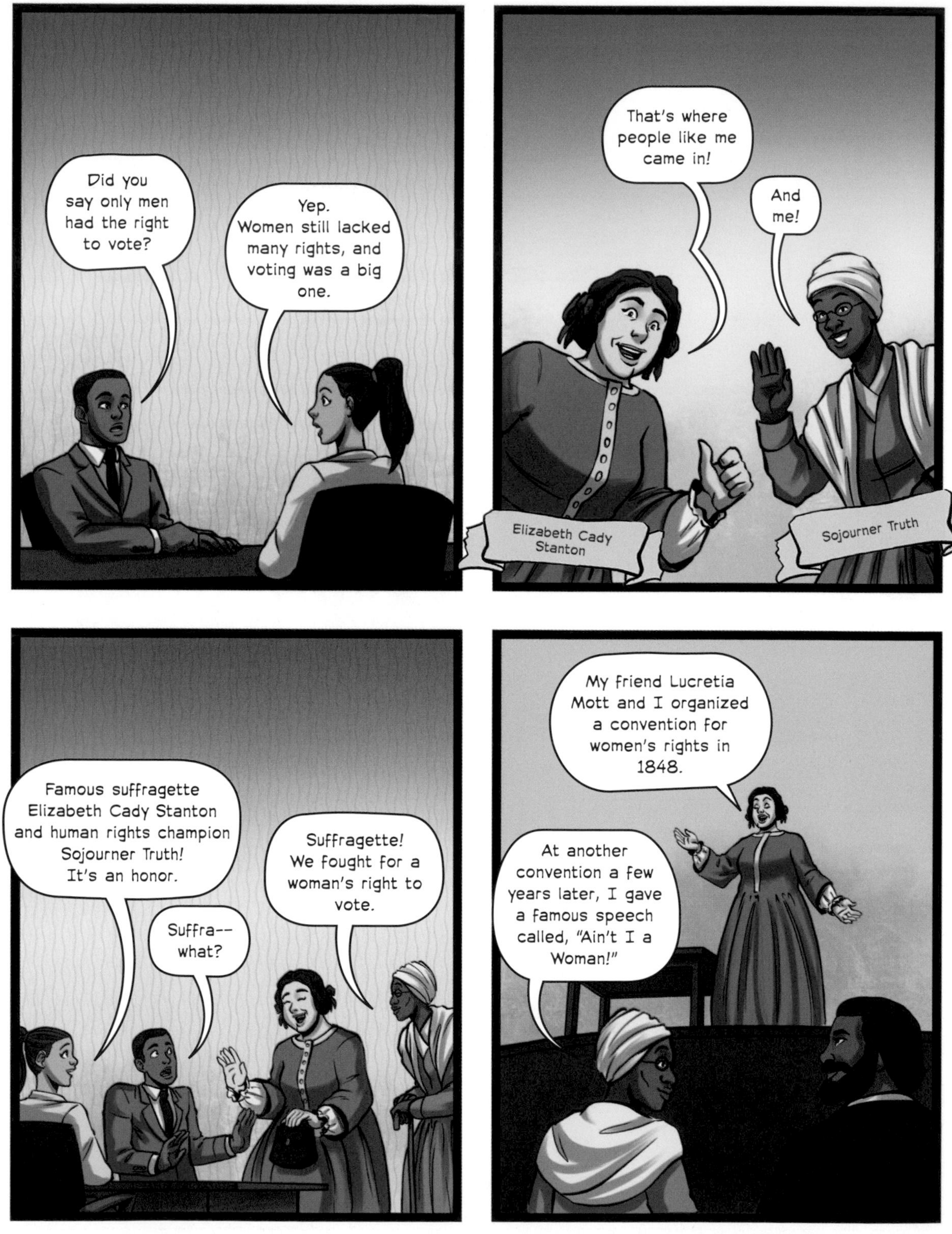
Did you say only men had the right to vote?
Yep. Women still lacked many rights, and voting was a big one.
That's where people like me came in!
And me!
Elizabeth Cady Stanton
Sojourner Truth
Famous suffragette Elizabeth Cady Stanton and human rights champion Sojourner Truth! It's an honor.
Suffra--what?
Suffragette! We fought for a woman's right to vote.
My friend Lucretia Mott and I organized a convention for women's rights in 1848.
At another convention a few years later, I gave a famous speech called, "Ain't I a Woman!"

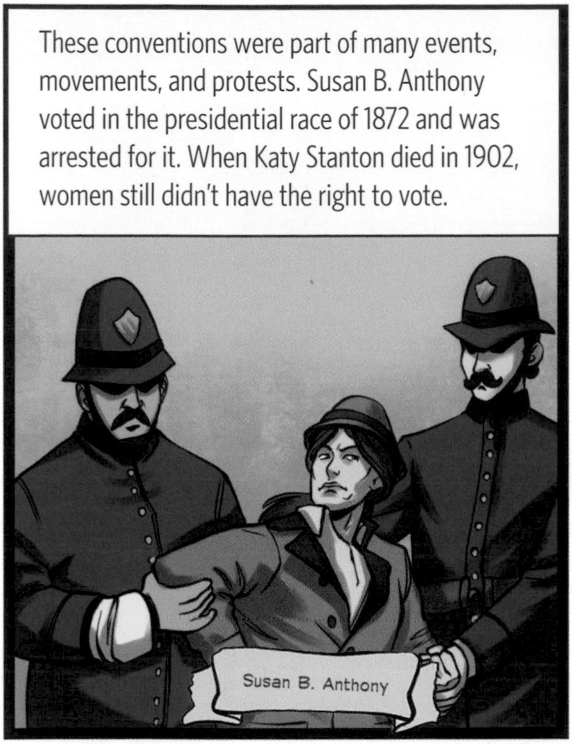
These conventions were part of many events, movements, and protests. Susan B. Anthony voted in the presidential race of 1872 and was arrested for it. When Katy Stanton died in 1902, women still didn't have the right to vote.
Susan B. Anthony

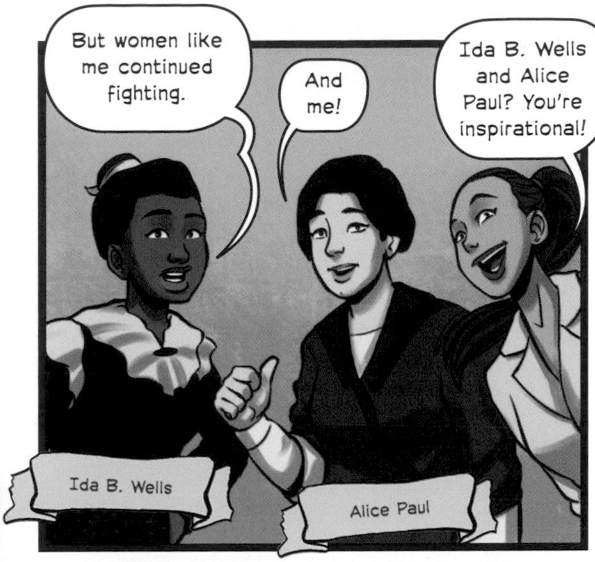
But women like me continued fighting.
And me!
Ida B. Wells and Alice Paul? You're inspirational!
Ida B. Wells
Alice Paul

PROGRESS IN THE STATES

Twenty states and territories gave women the right to vote before 1920. Jeannette Rankin was the first woman elected to Congress in 1916. She was a Republican congresswoman from Montana. Women there were given the right to vote in 1914.

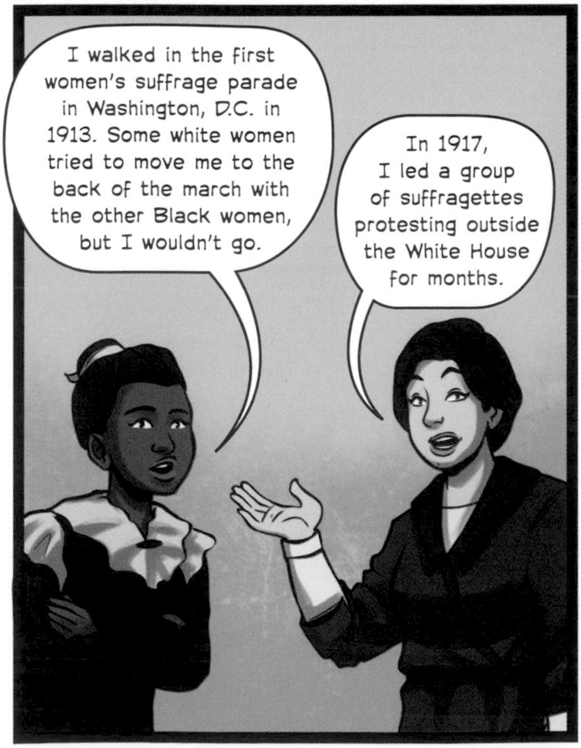
I walked in the first women's suffrage parade in Washington, D.C. in 1913. Some white women tried to move me to the back of the march with the other Black women, but I wouldn't go.
In 1917, I led a group of suffragettes protesting outside the White House for months.

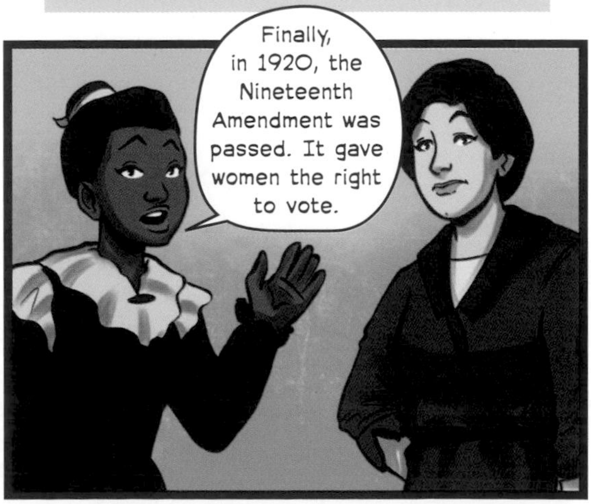
Finally, in 1920, the Nineteenth Amendment was passed. It gave women the right to vote.

CHAPTER FIVE: PARTY TIME

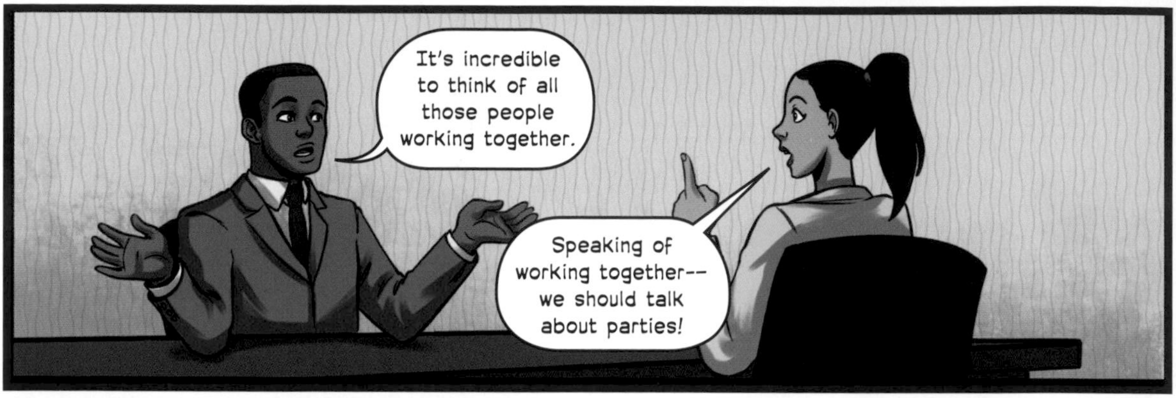
It's incredible to think of all those people working together.
Speaking of working together--we should talk about parties!

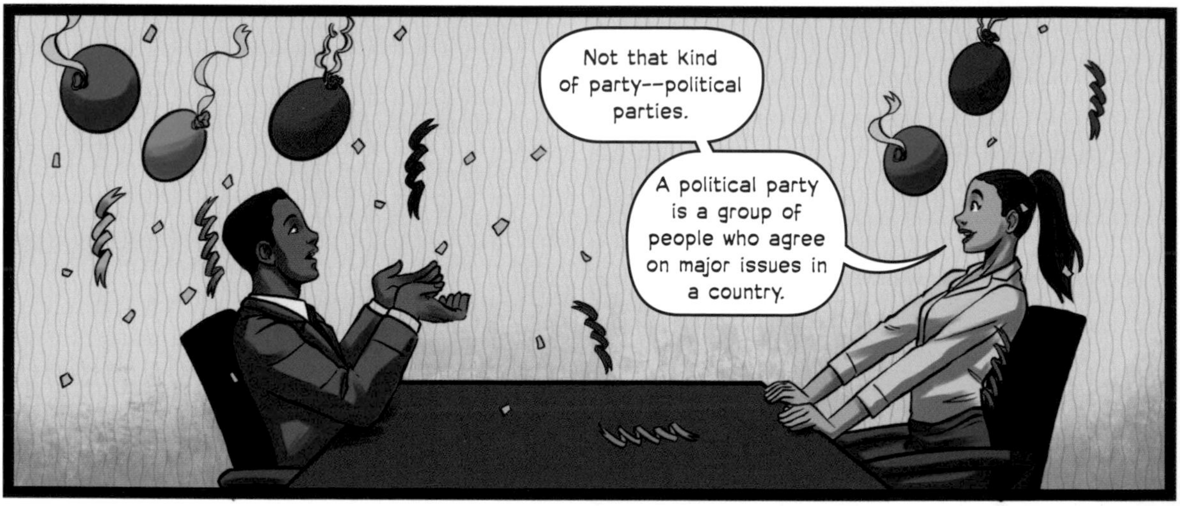
Not that kind of party--political parties.
A political party is a group of people who agree on major issues in a country.

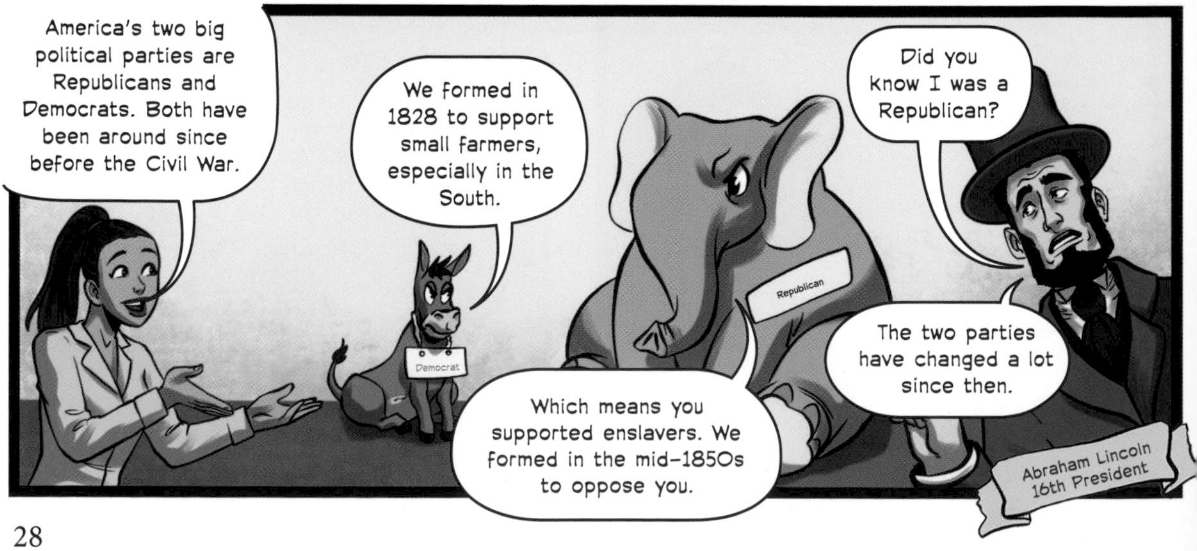
America's two big political parties are Republicans and Democrats. Both have been around since before the Civil War.
We formed in 1828 to support small farmers, especially in the South.
Democrat
Republican
Which means you supported enslavers. We formed in the mid-1850s to oppose you.
Did you know I was a Republican?
The two parties have changed a lot since then.
Abraham Lincoln
16th President

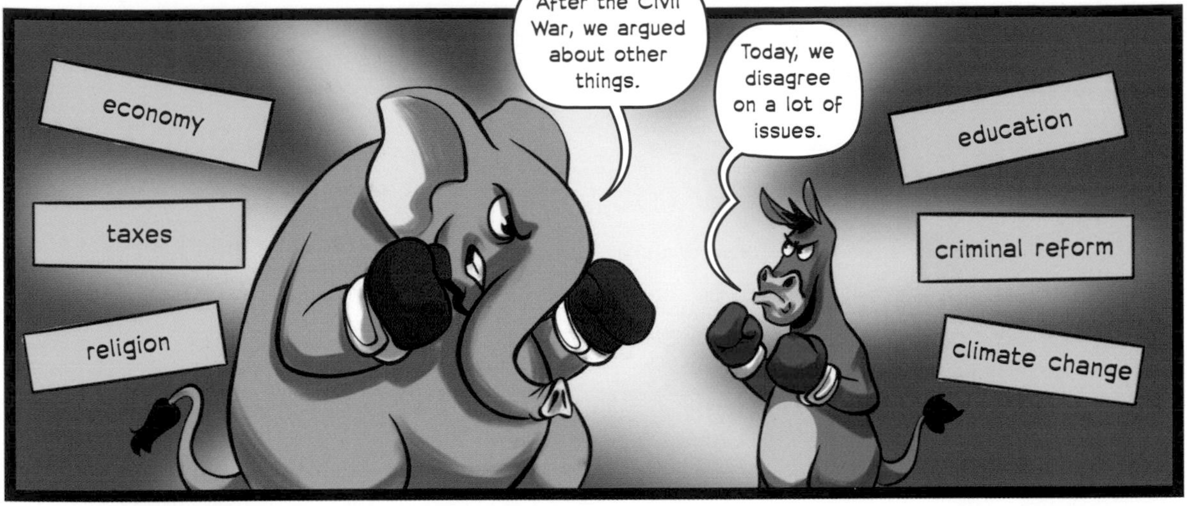
economy
taxes
religion
After the Civil War, we argued about other things.
Today, we disagree on a lot of issues.
education
criminal reform
climate change

FACT!

Any party outside of the Republicans and Democrats is called a "third party." Current third parties include the Green Party, which focuses on environmentalism, and the Libertarian Party. They want a smaller government.

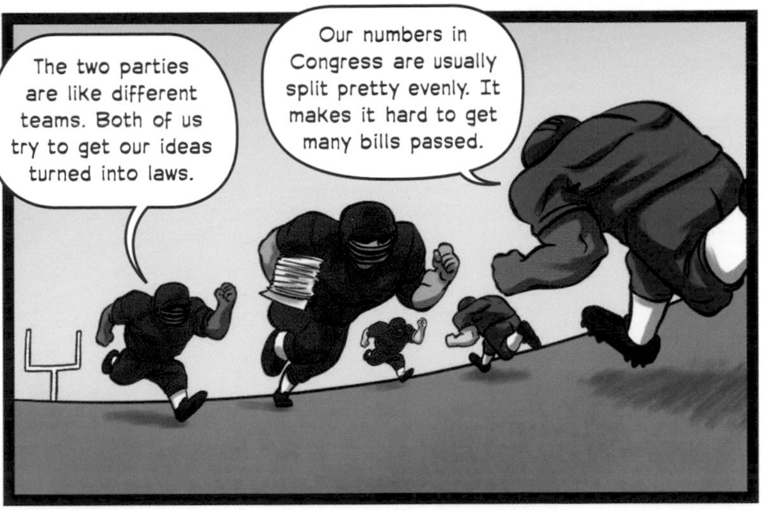
The two parties are like different teams. Both of us try to get our ideas turned into laws.
Our numbers in Congress are usually split pretty evenly. It makes it hard to get many bills passed.

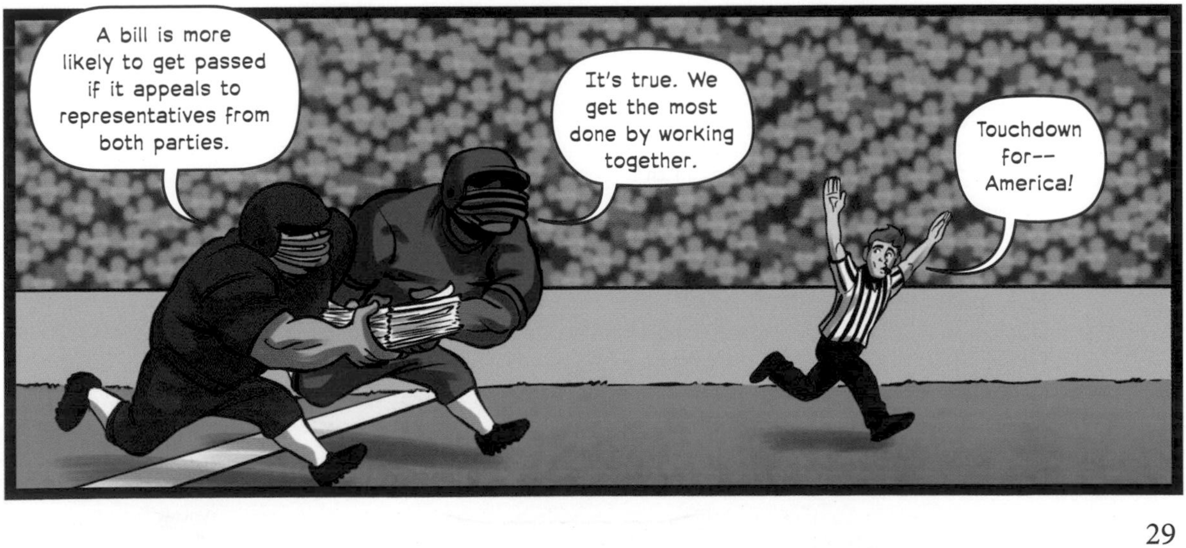
A bill is more likely to get passed if it appeals to representatives from both parties.
It's true. We get the most done by working together.
Touchdown for-- America!

GLOSSARY

amendment (uh-MEND-muhnt)—a formal change made to a law or legal document, such as the U.S. Constitution

bill (BIL)—a proposed law introduced in Congress

campaign (kam-PAYN)—organized actions and events carried out with the goal of being elected

candidate (KAN-duh-dayt)—a person who runs for office, such as president

census (SENN-suss)—an official count of all the people living in a country or district

delegate (DEL-uh-guht)—someone who represents other people at a meeting

elect (i-LEKT)—to choose someone as a leader by voting

electoral vote (i-lek-TOR-uhl VOHT)—a vote cast by the Electoral College, the group of people chosen by the voters to elect the president

filibuster (FILL-uh-bus-ter)—an effort to prevent action by making a long speech

legislature (LEJ-iss-lay-chur)—a group of elected officials who have the power to make or change laws for a country or state

subcommittee (SUB-kuh-mi-tee)—a small part of a larger group set up to deal with a particular issue

veto (VEE-toh)—to refuse to approve something from becoming a law; a president has the power to veto laws they do not support

READ MORE

Abramson, Jill. *What Is Congress?* New York: Penguin Workshop, 2021.

Bolinder, Mary Kate. *Leaders in Congress.* Huntington Beach, CA: Teacher Created Materials, 2022.

Woelfle, Gretchen. *A Take-Charge Girl Blazes a Trail to Congress: The Story of Jeannette Rankin.* New York: Calkins Creek, an imprint of Astra Books for Young Readers, 2023.

INTERNET SITES

Ben's Guide to the U.S. Government
bensguide.gpo.gov/

Fast Fact: United States Congress
newsforkids.net/fastfacts/united-states-congress/

Kids in the House: How a Bill Becomes a Law
kids-clerk.house.gov

ABOUT THE AUTHOR

Ted Anderson is a writer, librarian, and educator who lives in Minnesota. He has written original and licensed comics for multiple publishers, researched many interesting topics, and checked out thousands of books to eager readers.

ABOUT THE ILLUSTRATOR

Luiz Fernando da Silva is an illustrator and comic artist from Santa Catarina, Brazil. As a child, he created his own stories for fun, based on his favorite cartoons and video games. Luiz started his career as an illustrator and designer in 2006. He has been a full-time illustrator for more than 10 years. In his free time, he likes to watch movies and TV, play video games, read, and barbecue.